ISBN 978-1-334-35641-4
PIBN 10756696

# 1 MONTH OF
# FREE
# READING

## at
## www.ForgottenBooks.com

By purchasing this book you are eligible for one month membership to ForgottenBooks.com, giving you unlimited access to our entire collection of over 700,000 titles via our web site and mobile apps.

To claim your free month visit:
www.forgottenbooks.com/free756696

English
Français
Deutsche
Italiano
Español
Português

# www.forgottenbooks.com

**Mythology** Photography **Fiction**
Fishing Christianity **Art** Cooking
Essays Buddhism Freemasonry
Medicine **Biology** Music **Ancient
Egypt** Evolution Carpentry Physics
Dance Geology **Mathematics** Fitness
Shakespeare **Folklore** Yoga Marketing
**Confidence** Immortality Biographies
Poetry **Psychology** Witchcraft
Electronics Chemistry History **Law**
Accounting **Philosophy** Anthropology
Alchemy Drama Quantum Mechanics
Atheism Sexual Health **Ancient History**
**Entrepreneurship** Languages Sport
Paleontology Needlework Islam
**Metaphysics** Investment Archaeology
Parenting Statistics Criminology
**Motivational**

# Love-in-a-Mist

BY

POST WHEELER

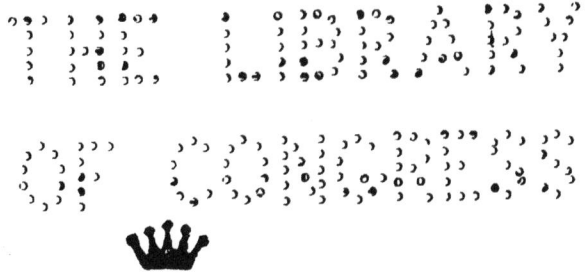

NEW YORK

THE CAMELOT COMPANY

1901

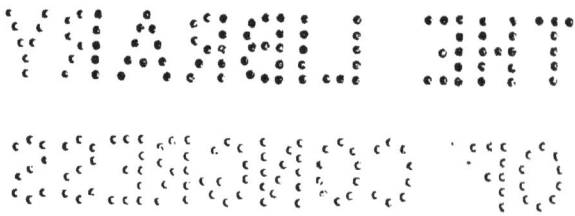

# TO ONE MOTHER.

When noiseless dusk wings down on pinions fleet,
  And, worn and wearied with their riotous play,
  The children leave their toys to long for day
And nod their heads in sleepiness complete,
The mother, all solicitous and sweet,
  Goes slowly up the balustraded way,
  Turning to hold the candle, so its ray
Shines down to guide the drowsy little feet.

So now I love to think you stand and wait
  Our stumbling footsteps up life's crooked stair,
    Letting love's candle shine down mother-wise,
While we, tired children! hasten (lest, if late,
  The fingered shadows seize us unaware)
    To see your placid age smile in our eyes.

# CONTENTS.

## MOSAICS.

## LOVE-IN-A-MIST.

## THE SINGING WIRE.

# CONTENTS.

## HARMONICS.

## THREE SONNETS.

## WHITE CLOVER.

## PASTELLES.

## ROCOCO.

## PALE LEAVES AND LILIES.

## RED LEAVES AND ROSES.

# CONTENTS.

# MOSAICS.

# THE TOAST.

The tapers wane, the chaplets pass,
   The dinner and the day are done;
Yet, ere we go, a final glass
   To a forgot, heroic one.
The glory of the golden bow
   Let petty poetasters trim.
What of the victor?   Well I know
   I owe no debt to Fate for him.

The great have greatness.   Let them be.
Gentlemen, standing!   Here's to ME!

The little master sups his woes,
   Flatters the hall above his ways;
Tricking obsequious brows, he goes
   In domino of neighbor's praise.
Up through the cloying periods' roll,
   The hidden tone speaks clear to us:
"A Noble, he!  (Behold, my soul,
      How generous I to laud him thus!)"

We sing our swelling brother high,
   Claim the low dust our own, and yet
The shackled and insensate " I "
   Laughs through the pigmy fume and sweat.
Unseen yet strenuous, behold,
   Behind the blare of pomp and pelf
Beneath the rags and cloth-of-gold,
   The eternal livery of Self!

I toast the " I " that mocks the " We "—
Ring you the crystal!   Here's to ME!

Within the mist that rules our chance,
   A clouded hand holds wreath and rod;
Yet see the little monads dance
   And wriggle in the grip of God!
For me—for ME life's game and plan!
   For ME the race beats slow or fleet.
I know no lord.   I am a man.
   I bring my deeds to my own feet.

The great of all the earth go by
   Anthemned and lauded by the mob.
The voice that cries them to the sky
   Dies out in silence and a sob.

## THE TOAST.

Kings, priests and Empires pass away,
 Behind the purple waits the shroud;
I—only I—am not of clay.
 He is a fool that talks so loud!

Myself is all my fief and fee.
Take you the offering. Here's to ME!

What of the far-off, blazoned name?
 The great desire, the spirit's wine,
The further dream, the sentient aim—
 These, these forever more, are mine!
Mine all world-joy and passing pain—
 All devious ways that spirit went!
Mine is the travail of the main,
 And mine the star-hung firmament!

I touch life's glass to you and Thee,
O Ever-Watching! Here's to ME!

# THE CHILD.

The mothers in fair Heaven,
   They gathered to the gate.
Their hair was free and hopefully
   Their brows were all elate.
They gathered in white, silent groups,
   And oh, not one was late.

Their tall, white thrones, upstanding,
   Smelled sweet with flowers in place
As still they passed and fixed their gaze
   On the far outer space—
A brooding gaze that caused to pass
   A dimness on God's face.

(It was the hour, at even,
   When the Great Angel tolls
The bell above the Sea of Glass
   And the broad gate unrolls
And up, like holy incense, come
   The little children's souls.)

# THE CHILD.

They stood all silent as they gazed
   Down the curved, purple zone,
To see, upon the hither side,
   By wandering meteors blown,
A tiny soul that up the ways,
   Came mounting all alone.

Red on the lonely waste it trod,
   By shadowy paths and far,
The golden hair burned all along
   Like to a tender star.
His little feet were white.   His eyes
   Were such as cherubs' are.

Each forward leaned a little space
   All warm and eager-eyed
To see him enter (one there was
   That had so lately died,
She held a hand against her heart
   And caught her breath and sighed).

Fresh blossoms pressed up to his breast
   Those slender hands of his.
(Oh, sweet!)   Their brooding gaze, bent on,
   So deep it grew, I wis,

That at the sight a trembling seized
　　The throne that Mary's is.

His baby face (it had no fear)
　　Was bright with first surprise.
He questioned each clear, placid look,
　　Trustful and searching-wise;
Then from them slowly turned away
　　His luminous, wide eyes.

One lingering gaze they gave as souls
　　By some blest view beguiled;
A shadow fell upon each face
　　That was so heavenly mild.
Each turned her, back to her fair throne,
　　And as they went, they smiled.

They shed no tear—no earthly ill
　　To that far glory strayed;
Yet at the smile (so sad it was)
　　The passing angels stayed,
And wondered in bright, shining rings,
　　Apart, and were afraid.

# HOPE.

Stone and weed,
   Flower and feather,
      Fin and wing and **man**—
All our need
   Winds together
      In The Plan.

Fire and star,
   Dust and spirit,
      Earth and You and **I**—
All that are
   I inherit
      In God's sky.

Heart, be brave!
   Mind, remember!
      Soul, attend the call!
Death's dulled grave,
   Love's ashed ember,
      Is not all.

# THE PRAYER.

*Our Father.*

　　　　　Hers.　She spoke it o'er and o'er
Just at the last, to that still look she wore,
Laying her wan hands together for a sign.
"Our Father"—aye, her Father, and so mine!


*Which art in Heaven.*

　　　　　　　Her place.　Thy stoniest hell
To clasp her would spring white with asphodel!
She touched it close as blessing touches prayer.
"In Heaven"—God's Heaven—my Heaven, for
　　she is there.


*Hallowed be Thy Name.*

　　　　　　　She spoke it so.　Her breath
Kissed it as worshiping softly, dear as death.
She deemed it holy—she; so would I call
The name that never tired her lips at all.

8

*Thy Kingdom come.*

     To me—to *me*, O Lord,
Who am so weary of this fire and sword,
Whose eyes are blinded and whose ears are dumb,
Life's end—and her! *To me* "Thy Kingdom
  come!"


*Thy will be done, on earth as it is in Heaven.*
For her the winds walked, and the stars at even.
Are the winds thine, and shall her saddened place
Dim Thy bright throne with longing for my face?


*Give us this day our daily bread.*
       Oh, sweet!
Give me to kiss her hair, her hands, her feet!
She was my soul's wine all that blessed while.
Give me, for my heart-hunger, but her smile!


*Forgive us our trespasses.*
      Oh, I know
I was not always tender! Be it so.
A word I might have said—a slighted kiss—
She would—and yet—(nay, God, forgive not this!).

*As we forgive*

   (She hoarded up no wrong!)

*Them that trespass against us.*

      Her soul song

Was keyed to kindness. Never did she pine,

Never remembered any hurt of mine.


*And lead us not into temptation.*

     Such

As comes sometimes to those who suffer much.

This worn husk wearies me — Death wears no

  frown—

Tempt me not with the thought to lay it down!


*Deliver us from evil.*

    Lord, I show

No bane, no sickness, save in suffering so.

I bear Thee no weak ills, no specious tear—

My evil only that she is not here!


*For Thine is the Power and Glory.*

     What are we,

Angels and men and bleeding things like me?

The Power, Thou hast—the power that takes away;
And Glory—that was mine but yesterday!


*Forever and ever.*
     Can her watching face
Not ever turn from Thy far, holy place?
O Lord, in Thy forever, once again
Give her to me! Give her to me!

        AMEN!

Oh, little Christ-Child, I have children three.
    (Hush! Did you start, little brother?)
Oh, little Christ-Child, I have children three,
Jean and Margot and p'tite Marie,
    Who pray to thee and thy mother.
Oh, little Christ-Child, they are pure and good.
They have loved thee always as they should.
    (Hush! Did you cry, little brother?)

Oh, little Christ-Child, and the fever high!
    (Hush! Did you moan, little brother?)
Oh, little Christ-Child, all heart am I!
Send thy angel away—let him pass me by,
    For the love and the tears of thy mother!
Oh, little Christ-Child, of my lambkins three,
My sick little one—is he least to me?
    (Hush! Did you moan, little brother?)

Oh, Little Christ-Child—and my bird in its nest!
    (Hush! Do you breathe, little brother?)
Oh, little Christ-Child—and the first on my breast!
Thou art angry because I have giv'n thee no rest—
    Thou and thy holy white mother!
Oh, little Christ-Child—and his eyes were so sweet!
His little, thin arms and his poor, weak feet!
    (Hush! You are cold, little brother!)

## SESTINA.

In every day the sunshine of her eyes,
In every night the darkness of her hair!
   I see her when the morning comes in fire,
   When the slow eve falls over my desire,
And the long dark that empties out my sighs.
In every day the sunshine of her eyes.

In every night the darkness of her hair,
In every moon the glory of her smile!
   I know no time, no happening, no place,
   No sleep, no waking, save but by her face,
Nor any thought at all but she is there.
In every night the darkness of her hair.

In every moon the glory of her smile,
In every leaf the whisper of her feet!
   Oh, life could hold no other joy than this—
   To know the prison of her arms and kiss
That I have wanted all this weary while.
In every moon the glory of her smile.

In every leaf the whisper of her feet!
Day's brightness and night's shadow and moon's
    smile,
  All intimate of Her! Dear Death, how still
  The world is when it's empty! 'Neath the hill
That little stone! And how my pulses beat!
In every leaf the whisper of her feet!

# THE HUELESS VALE.

I came in sleep within a vale
    Deep set and lapped in quietness.
Its sky stretched colourless and pale
    And its hillsides were lustreless.
And over it a droning wind
    Went sorrowing for its vanished smile,
As some worn woman who hath sinned
    In dreaming, sobs the while.

Down dropped the sickly blossoms white,
    Half blown, from boughs as starved as they;
The yellow leaves, bit off with blight,
    Deep-rustling in the wood-ways lay.
The very grass stood gaunt and thin,
    Gray, seedless, sedge-like, parched and sere,
And all those pallid haunts within
    No bird-note could I hear.

There, as I passed, I came between
    Twin hillocks, to a place, I wis,

Of long dead souls.   Ten worlds had seen
   None other place that sighed like this!
For all the hollowed paths were strown,
   Limb-locked and writhing, lean and pied,
With ghosts that made that weary moan
   Nor lifted voice beside.

Wan, starveling souls with lips agrin,
   Sad souls with sighs all odorous,
Pale souls with eyes the colour of sin
   And lips for kisses amorous,
Outstretched they lay or half upraised
   And stared me from their gloomy bed,
Like some mad city, spelled and mazed
   To mock the buried dead.

Then, as I gazed, a wavering cry
   Shrilled out, as, seven days after death,
From new-made grave is heard the sigh
   Of its fierce soul that wrestleth.
"Behold!" it said, "for we are they
   Who all our lives long sought but this—
To hug the jewel of world-display
   And recked not who Love is!

" Here in this vale of lack-desire
   We linger, dolorous and distraught,
Praying to know his holy fire,
   Whom glad Love ne'er had known nor taught.
Here bideth such as did despite
   To Love and did betray his name,
Reft from the garden of false delight,
   Our roses touched with flame!"

# THE BROKEN REGIMENT.

"Is our flag flaunting?
  Or do they bear it low?
And where are all the columns
  That we watched so?"

      "Lad, the flag is drooping;
        Look, and you will see.
      The minute gun is firing—
        What is that to me?"

"Is our flag waving?
  Or is it draped with woe?
And where are all the comrades
  That we loved so?"

      "Lad, the flag is weeping,
        The drum is muffled, too.
      The minute gun is booming—
        What is that to you?"

15

"Is our flag flying,
   And goes it toward the foe?
  And where are all the boys-in-blue
  That we cheered so?"

  "Lad, the flag is flying!
    'Twill fly forever thus!
  The minute gun is silent—
  What is that to us?"

# THE CRY OF THE MAN.

The cry of the Man—
"God, give me Soul!
A body I have;
Thy life I inherit.
Grant now unto me
An immortal Spirit!
I reach—I aspire.
The evermore higher
Is beyond and denied me.
Give me Soul, God, or hide me
From mountains and sea
And Thy mighty wind
And fear that they nourish!
Has my voice angered Thee?
God, have I sinned?
And shall I now perish?"

And God gave Man Soul.

The cry of the Man—
" God, give me Love!
    A spirit I have,
      A Soul to uphold me.
    Grant now unto me
      A Love to enfold me!
I long—I am lonely.
Thy wide Content only
  Is forever denied me.
  Give me Love, God, or hide me
    From nest-song of birds,
      And dumb forest mating,
        And whelps the brutes cherish!
  Art Thou wroth at my words
    To view me with hating?
      And shall I now perish? "

And God gave Man Love.

# THE GUIDE.

*" This is thy burden.     Yet an hour,*
*    And the poor pain shall pass !"*
The words come dropping like a shower
    Through heat the sun's day has,
To my soul, set, a lone lamped tower,
    Where mist-things pass and pass.

Dreaming, I walk beyond the night
    Whence the clear mystery stirs,
And wonder if, in some long light,
    I shall know smile of hers.
For light were dark without that sight,
    And life than death were worse.

*" All this shall end.     Thy waiting cheek*
*    Shall flush to hers !"*     Oh, Thine !
I wake to hear that calm Voice speak
    To a sunk ear of mine.
My heart that, hoping, will not break,
    Leans far out for a sign.

She had a smile (God knows!) that sung
   Like a stretched silver wire.
Her look rose upward, straight and young,
   Like a gold, slender spire.
Her kiss was like a pale flower hung
   On the dusk wall of desire.

Her face has lighted all my ways.
   Now that my tears are blown
In my dimmed eyes' uncertain haze,
   Dear God! Is she Thine own?
Shall she at Thy Throne stay to praise
   While I wend on alone?

" *On thy glad breast shall her sweet eyes*
   *Fold down. So shalt thou know!* "
Thou who hast framed all mysteries,
   Shall this fall even so?
Now she is made all heaven-wise,
   Wilt Thou yet bid her go?

She sorrowed meekly when she sinned,
   And gave mild tongue to Thee;
But when she grieved me, a fierce wind
   Tore at her spirit's sea.

At my shut heart her full sobs dinned—
  Thus, God, she cared for me!

Thou hast slain men (by the Wise Book)
  With Thy great lightning stirred;
I could have stabbed her by a look,
  And slain her with a word.
Yet was I loath, as Christ had shook
  To kill a nesting bird.

" *Thou shalt go forth, not yet to wrath.*
  *She shall go forth, and free!* "
I hear the whisper.  Still my path
  Doth point wide out from Thee.
Give me this dream that such joy hath—
  That she shall fare with me!

I will tread softer, better, so—
  For look on her still face.
" *She shall stay for thee!* "  Far and low
  I hear it down the ways.
One day together we shall go
  Back to her God, for grace.

# ARMS OF THE UNFORGOT.

Long not for Love.    Look not for Love at all.
Pray not to see her—ever to hear her cry
When it goes by upon the wind.    Bow down!
Hide thy face from her, lest her tyrannous eyes
Steal from thee all the pictures of thy soul!

For Love is fine and tense as silver wire,
Fierce as white lightning, glorious as drums,
And beautiful as snow-mountains.    Swift she is
As leaping flame and calm as winter stars.
He whom she calls must lift his face and follow,
Follow forever, never knowing rest,
Mixed of all ecstasies, barren of all peace,
Reaching and thrusting, keen as dusty thirst—
And find her in the hollow of his days,
Gone shrunken, formless, rattling, and as dry
As three-day ashes on a pulpy heath.
Follow her not, I say!
                    Hark!    Didst thou hear
A sudden singing?

                    Oh, and is it Thou?
Stay for me but a breath!    Pass Thou not on!
I run—I run—O, lift me to Thy lips!

25

# THE TROOPER.

"Soldier, soldier, out of the South,
Bring you mourning for my mouth?
   Your face is sad, your eyes are dim.
   Where in the blue veldt laid ye him?"

"Mother, mother, oh, we were few!
Out in the wide veldt, bare and blue,
   Where an hundred helmeted troopers fell,
   There in his blanket he sleeps well!"

"Soldier, soldier, give me your hand!
Fought he well in that stubborn land?
   Here at home he was wild and bad.
   Rode he well for the Queen, my lad?"

"Mother, mother, he spurred between
And gave me his body for a screen."
   "Thank God, soldier! Never gave he
   His body between the world and me!"

# DE GUSTIBUS.

Out of the depths, Mother—out of the depths!
  *The sadness of slow living!*  Heed my sigh.
  I am so humble and thou art so high.
  Bend down and listen, for—I die!—I die!
Mother of all, and Mother of me—my Mother.

Out of the depths, Mother—out of the depths!
  *The leanness of desire!*  Oh, hear my cry.
  Lean out and look upon me where I lie.
  Bend down and hear me, for—I die!—I die!
Mother of all, and Mother of me—my Mother.

Out of the depths, Mother—out of the depths!
  *The pain of love in darkness!*  Turn thine eye.
  Bend down from out of thy implacable sky.
  Bend down and save me, for—I die!—I die!
Mother of all, and Mother of me—my Mother.

# SONNET.

Change—change is death.  The forms we treasure
   here
  Slip wraithlike, weeping, into pallid night,
  To bless, ah, never, never more, our sight,
And leave each heart to hold an empty bier.
Listen.  A babe was born.  With its first tear
  The mother slept, life's sweet, warm-lettered
   light
  Dead in her eyes.  The child grew, fair and white,
To make rare music for my youth's love year.

She, too, has gone.  I loved her.  Had she stayed
  She might have known a son who, closing down
   The wearied lids, had cried with sobbing
    breath,
Kissing the brow where age its lines had laid.
  O mother soul, your babe!  O youth!  O son!
   Can she be yours?  I tell you, change is death!

# COMING OF DARK.

Sweet eyes, sweet lips, sweet hair with sunlight
   woven—
Ah, life to show me love were sure behoven!
Pale hands, soft heart, low voice and kiss at even—
Were this but all, my world would yield me heaven.
      (Ah, no!   There is no night!)

Sweet eyes—why has the light their depths for-
   saken?
Sweet lips—has dark their riper radiance taken?
Not now are their low tendernesses spoken.
Sweet hair—the last sun-shaft has fallen broken.
      (No, no!   *'Tis not the night?*)

To clasp no more—white hands!—in lovers' meet-
   ing!
To feel no more—still heart!—the pulses beating!
O voice that called me from all trivial hating—
O kiss that lisps around me, shivering, waiting—
      (*God! God!   It is the night!*)

# A PRAYER AT NIGHT.

Now, at the end, I lay me down to sleep,
   From all my little delving in the sand.
I pray the Lord still, still, my soul to keep,
   Along my journeying to another land,
Warm from the tempest and the further deep—
(Now, at the end, I lay me down to sleep).

If I, perchance, should die before I wake,
   If there wait chasms dark and Lethes dim,
I pray the Lord, who knows, my soul to take
   Safe through the voids between this life and Him,
And lift me, at the last, for my soul's sake—
(If I, perchance, should die before I wake).
                 Amen!

# LOVE IN-A-MIST.

# ASHED ALTARS.

You whom I gave my longing and ambition,
   My toil, my treasure and my meed of Art,
Who blessed my good and prayèd my sin's remis-
    sion,
   Take you this song and lay it on your heart.

It is all pale, not red as is first passion,
   Weary and broken, sad for sorrow's part,
Moving unjoyful, tricked in sober fashion.
   Take you this song and lay it on your heart.

You knew the fire, the sun-blaze, the fruition;
   Now the grey snows lie o'er the tendrils' start.
Shall spring again rain down in tears' contrition?
   Take you this song and lay it on your heart.

Lay it there wistful, in a sweet confusion,
   Dreaming it smiles, that thro' its veins there dart
Tongues of dead heat, the sparks of old illusion—
   Take you this song and lay it on your heart.

## BEYOND.

God knows—God knows the thing I wish for most!
  'Tis such a little thing, so mean and small
  As the world deems it, but my all in all,
My diadem, my glory and my boast.

God knows—God knows why it will never be—
  Never can pass my way, and yet—and yet—
  Oh, if it should! If this dear thing were set
Near, nearer, no king's kiss were aught to me!

# THE WAYFARERS.

A little way, my dear, a little way
    Along rough roads, in valleys gloomiest—
A little way of storm and bitter day,
    And then the sweet home-harbour and the rest.

A little way, my dear, a little way
    Of wish deferred and hope grown tremulous—
A little way of doubt and wanting grey,
    And then the fireside and the kiss for us.

A little way, my dear, a little way
    Sown with life's tears, with all love's flowers
        blown old—
A little way—and then the opening May,
    The further vision, and the Gate of Gold.

# WRECKS.

Just one small light between me and the dark.
   Just one small heart between the gale and me.
One soft, small hand to guide my yawing bark
   Across strange wastes of all uncharted sea.

I cannot think how, if the light should fail!
   I dare not dream how, if that heart were cold.
Nor how to harbour through the gloom and gale
   Were that small hand to loose its rudder hold!

God will not let it be!　And yet—and yet—
   To-night a battered hulk drove ghostly by,
Wind-broken, helmless, with her bent prow set
   Hard for the rocks between the sea and sky.

# DOUBT.

Oh, she must be all in all to me,
   And I must be all to her that's true.
This is my gospel.   Let it be.
   Nothing else will do.

Rival of mine I will never know!
   Why should two of us bend and bow?
All hearts come to their masters.   So
   Hers must know me now.

Other loves may have been her fate—
   (Women know where they love the best!)—
But mine must be so great, so great,
   It will swallow all the rest.

Other loves—she may cling to them,
   But unless I can be her all in all,
Till my one love stays as her diadem,
   I will not be hers at all!

# THE MOON-OF-BRIGHT-NIGHTS.

The frail, curved, golden bubble of the moon
  Hangs up above the boughs and a one star,
Pale as a lily in a heated noon,
  Trails wanly where no clustering comrades are.
The little leaves hang down; the winds are dead.
Put your lips nearer.   What was that you said?

I know, I know.   The world would say so, sweet—
  The watching world that knows its business best,
The world that never clasped your pretty feet
  Nor stroked your neck's curve, down from chin
    to breast,
Here in the fog-dew, with the summer old.
Did you sigh then?   Why—why, your lips are cold!

Draw closer yet.   (Ah, do not sob, my heart!)
  Press not the thorn of our wild-rose desire.
Your sob is spear-sharp, piercing like a dart
  My soul that's wound with love and mist and fire.
Kiss me again.   The little star is bright.
The moon swings low.   Ah, grieve not so to-night.

# IF SHE SHOULD SOMETIMES SAY A PRAYER FOR ME.

If she should sometimes say a prayer for me—
   If, when the daylight pales and fades and dies,
   And sleep becks smilingly to her sweet eyes,
She should but breathe my poor name, trustingly!

For I have dreamed that she, her tender knees
   Pressed on the carpet, and her arms outspread,
   Warming with her white breast the coverlid,
Draws to her all pure angels that God sees.

I am not good, as she is, for her grace
   Is all things innocent, and all things fair.
   I had not known what men might be and dare,
Until my Self looked up and saw her face.

But now—I dare to dream that I might be,
   Perhaps, who have been idle in the earth,
   Something more noble, something better worth—
If she should sometimes say a prayer for me.

# CONFESSION.

Dear, I could tell you many sins of mine,
　Sins of hot hand, proud heart and love amiss.
Could you forgive them, then were love divine;
　Could you forget them, love were more than this.

More than this clasp, this kiss, this clinging touch;
　More than this earth has taught its children here.
You would forgive me—have forgiven much—
　Ah, but I know you'd not forget them, dear!

Ask me no more.　Your little heart is kind.
　I will repent, but I could never see
That hurt look in your eyes that turns them blind,
　That quick curve on your lips that have kissed
　　me!

Though for a moment—though it trembled out
　Into sad smiles, though eyes looked mild again—
Still for that moment love would dim with doubt;
　I should be just a man with other men.

Now I am more.   I sit above the rest
   Secure, enthroned (though undeserving quite),
And feel the sweet fire kindle in your breast,
   And see your eyes shine through my dreams at
     night.

Shall I risk this my kingdom?   Shall I show
   My soul before it stood up straight and tall?
Think me not sinless—there were sins—but oh,
   You still can smile and deem them passing small.

## SPRING.

Oh, my beloved, when spring is really come,
  We know it not by thrush's meadow note,
Or wind's leaf-laughter or waked insect's hum,
  Nor by the robin with his crimson coat—

Not by pale bloodroot, standing in the wood,
  The first arbutus or the sound of bees,
Nor the new fronds where autumn bracken stood,
  Nor silver-velvet buds on willow trees.

No—but we know it when the heart beats fast,
  When the warm tears stand in the eyelid's door,
When in the throat a something rises fast
  At thought of days that were but are no more.

# THE DEMON OF THE SHADOW.

At night I often think, "If she were dead!"
   Half-waking and in anguished afterwhile
   I strain my blinded eyes to see her smile,
And my tense ear to hear her coming tread.

My life rings wildly, fools itself with fears,
   With cheat of endless guessing—dreams that
      start
   In that white "if" that ices on my heart,
That "one day" that must mock my mood to tears.

Beyond—Oh, God!—the darkness lies so deep!
   Lift thou the thought. Let me forget Death's
      frown
   A little time! Let me not lay me down
Night after night to sob my soul to sleep!

## A DREAM OF LAST NIGHTS.

I saw the billowed cushions 'neath her head,
  The strait, kind vestments, clasping fold and fold,
Pale lips I never thought to see but red,
  And gleams of hair in silent whorls of gold.

And I laid little kisses on her eyes
  And I set pale-blue orchids in her hair.
Meseemed that day that only Death was wise
  And love a vagrant bubble in the air.

# INDIFFERENCE.

There was small reason in our quarrel.  My part
   Perhaps was greater.  Long I lay awake,
With cheek hot on the pillow and my heart
   Sore with its beating, stubborn in its ache.

Still but unquiet, each nerve tense to hark
   The little, whispered love-things that I missed,
My smarting eyes wide open on the dark—
   So fell the first night that we had not kissed.

I could have prayed reproaches, longed for tears,
   For sweet, hurt sobbing where the shadows crept,
But bitterer far to tremble to my ears,
   The calm, low breathing that betrayed she slept.

# THE LATE REPLY.

Ah me, when I was her all-in-all!
    (Blind, blind!)  A man is a sightless stone.
Those colourless days beyond recall
    And each of us here alone!

Dead her tenderest thoughts that were,
    Ne'er to be born my joys to be;
And I am nothing, nothing to her
    As she was nothing to me.

We know and we see when it is too late.
    (She knew, but ah, in time love dies so.)
I think the bitterest things of fate
    The devil cannot know.

Or else in hell there will still be space
    For love to wander and weary not
Till late love, coming too late to its place,
    May find itself forgot.

But oh, the all that I was to her,
    And the endless all that she is to me—
To be only a dust of the things that were
    And a ghost of the things that be!

# THE QUARREL.

My dear came to me, bending down her head,
  Her breast quick rising and her sweet voice
    quaking,
To ask forgiveness for some word she said
  When her sad heart was aching.

And at her voice (for mine had been the making
  Of this poor quarrel that clouded board and bed)
My throat swelled, all my sullenness forsaking.

I could not speak at once.   Then my soul bled
  Into a great, round sob, and, her calm breaking,
Swiftly she knelt and my lips comforted
  With lips where love lay waking.

# TENDERNESS.

I hurt you, dear, the other day.    I smiled
   When I should have seemed sorry; or I jarred
   Your weaker mood with tone unused and hard,
Forgetting, quite, the future and the child.

But when I saw your little lips shake fast,
   Your eyelids redden so, and the big drops
   Splash on your wrists—I felt as one who stops
His hand to see a redbreast gasp its last,

Or strikes a small doll-mother for her fears,
   Or robs a little cripple of his crutch—
   So careless was my heart that cared so much,
So tender was the spot that felt your tears!

# THE LETTER.

"Till I come home again," the letter ran,
    And signed, "Your darling" (one word else,
      maybe),
And in between, the visit, how began,
    With something of her loneliness for me.

More of the weather, asking of me not
    To let her tulip die—to find her ring—
To wrap my throat, which I, manlike, forgot,
    And many another little foolish thing.

You know what women's letters are! and this,
    Hurriedly written, winging swiftly back,
Was just another sent to me to kiss,
    Dear beyond telling—dear for very lack.

If I should die to-day and this were found
    Laid carefully, in-buttoned, heart above,
Perhaps some lips would smile and eyes around
    Would wonder at the childishness of love.

But, oh, there would be some who, swallowing hard,
    Would turn away with quick smart of a tear,
And (passing on to some loved life they guard)
    Would know why this slim scribbled page is dear!

# THREE KISSES.

When first I kissed you, 'twas full on your mouth,
  Red as a blackbird's cherry.   You recall;
'Twas spring, the soft air smelling of the South,
  The whole world gay and you gay most of all.
You laughed—that low, sweet, tender, birdlike trill
Which made the very bobolink be still.

When next I kissed you, 'twas upon the cheek,
  Molded just round enough.   'Twas autumn then
And you were graver grown, and did not speak,
  But seemed in wonder at the ways of men.
And yet you smiled.   So dear a smile it was
That it seemed sudden summer over us.

When last I kissed you, dearest heart of gold,
  My lips just brushed your forehead.   You were
     sad,
And it was winter.   All the world was old.
  But at the touch, my love swelled fierce and glad;
For then I felt you tremble, and saw fall
Two great slow tears.   Ah, that was best of all.

# PRESCIENCE.

My love who loved me better than my dreaming,
  Came to my side one night, and by the bed,
In the wide moonlight bar a wraith-shape seeming,
  Caught at my coverlid;
Knelt with a sudden clasping and a crying
Never a word to my first words replying.

Then, when her speech came, sadly worn and
    broken,
  Said she knew not how such a folly fell;
Nothing she guessed of grief or evil token;
  "Perhaps she was not well";
Soothed my concern, then laughed 'mid her own
    sighing
And so stole back and left me wakeful lying.

It stood a puzzle then.  But on a morrow
  I looked upon her thro' dim eyes and felt
The thrill of that same tender prescient sorrow
  That wrung her when she knelt.
And then I knew that 'twas her soul went crying,
Hearing God's faint, far whisper of her dying.

# TRUST.

She could not trust my hand when, in the street,
   We threaded devious ways amid the press;
But dread of wheel and hoof-beat led her feet
   This way, then that, in turnings purposeless.
And when, so speeding, she escaped my arm
   To miss, by but a hair, the pounding dray,
Why, when I saw how intimate the harm,
   I chided and was angry, in man's way.

But when, one night, the King of Terrors spurred
   His ghastly steed across my treasure-land,
Those who watched nearest, hardly breathing, heard
   Her sob, "If he could only hold my hand!
O God, dear God!—I would not be afraid!"
   And I, quick summoned, hasting from the deep,
Saw but her smile as, sobbing o'er, she laid
   Her hand in mine, and trusting, fell asleep.

# WHEN I GO HOME.

If she were there, when I went home to-night—
   If I should see her form against the wall,
Her hair all tangled rosy with the light,
   Startled to hear my key grate in the hall—

If she should spring against me, just the same
   As in those days (ah, love so tender is!)
My face set in her white arms' oval frame,
   And all her body bending to my kiss—

If she should stand thus, silent, loving so,
   Her little fingers clasping on my head,
And I could feel her soft breath come and go
   Bending my ear for first low words she said—

If she were there—God knows why she is not!
   (They say He knows, who ache for no dear thing.)
I only know my heart is hurt and hot!
   I only know the fierceness and the sting!

# THE AFTERWARD.

Quite calmly now I view it at the last,
  The upper room where all her pains were done,
And, the long bitter and the anguish past,
  Recall those few, fond meetings, one by one.

There is the window where she used to sit,
  Humming, low-voiced, some foolish woman's
    song.
There hangs her mirror, in the depths of it
  No shadow of dear eyes it knew so long.

I mind me when she pinned that picture there,
  And when she brought that horseshoe from the
    street—
Oh, I could close my eyes and smell her hair,
  Almost—almost, could think I heard her feet!

But it is gone and life is warm and wide.
  And I am calm.   See, here's her closet door.
So.——God!   That smell of flowers the day she
    died!
  And here—O, Christ!—The little gown she
    wore!

# THE EMPTY DWELLING.

See, through the day, the sweetness of the sun!
 See, through the heat, the comfort of the shade!
They lay, past days, for each his other one,
 Who now 'neath sun and shadow low are laid.

And one—my one—laughed often loud and long.
 And one—your one—smiled often at your knee.
Now they are gone from summer and from song;
 The sky and shade clasp only you and me.

See how the buds hang bursting on the boughs!
 See how the bloodroot peeps from out the mould!
The bud and flower once gloried all the house
 Set by small hands that now are folded cold.

And one—your one—loved best the apple-bloom.
 And one—my one—chose lily-bells for me.
Now only dust through echoing hall and room;
 The flowers blow on—the buds hang on the tree.

See, in my eyelash, dims a one wet tear!
 See, on your cheek, its fellow lonely lies!
We understand.  'Tis fair in summer here—
 I could not bear it when the autumn dies!

# THE UNLAID GHOST.

We sit at the table—that other and I·
    Between us the glitter of glass and of plate.
The jest and the wine and the tale go by,
    Till over the walnuts the hour grows late.

We smile at each other across the ferns,
    The gleam of the rose-shade tinges her face.
And something deep in me kindles and burns
    When her slim throat pulses its yellow lace.

Where in my brain was that ghost of a sob?
    She?   Ah, never again, I know!
If only I could not see that throb,
    Like the breast of a caught bird, frightened so!

Queer, how a trick of a vein will bring
    Dead memory down like a waterfall.
The quivering, unforgettable thing
    Is such a little thing, after all!

A thing that a casual eye must miss—
 A bit of old lace, with the little stir
Of the white skin under—only this—
 But, oh, how it always belonged to her!

"Dead," did I say? (How unlined her brow!)
 Dead? Ah, that is for her—but I—
Something stirred in my heart just now—
 Something I buried too deep to die.

Bravo! This is as good as a play!
 Fool! To breathe hard at the sight of a face!
But, oh, to smile—and the terrible way
 Her throat will pulse in that yellow lace!

# THE LITTLE FLOWERS UPON HER BREAST THAT DIED.

One day (strange, strange how subtle odours cling!)
    They sang and shut her face from the sweet air.
On the rich velvet my poor little ring—
    They said—glowed with the glory of her hair.
I conned the name the silver letters spelled.
    They came and touched and whispered me and
      cried.
My eyes were dead.   My nostrils only smelled—
    The little flowers upon her breast that died!


To-day I sat and watched the passing throng.
    A sad, grey sky was dropping sadder rain;
And yet I heard a teamster's careless song,
    And knew that time was kind to cover pain.
The steeples clangoured as the midhour belled.
    A sudden jest caught up—how like! I sighed.
I felt the rain, and all at once I smelled—
    The little flowers upon her breast that died!

# THE TREASURE.

I dreamed—since she had passed from me
　　From my poor cot and humble place,
And that I wandered restlessly
　　And ne'er might see her face—

I dreamed fair other faces came,
　　Drawn in sweet lines, to hold me dear;
That other hands held just the same,
　　Struck new tunes for my ear.

I dreamed they filled me to the brim,
　　Against my love, against my will;
That the fierce sorrow faded dim
　　And my soul's grief lay still.

I dreamed that she came back and stood,
　　With tears upon her pale, small face,
Sobbing as stilly as she could,
　　And watched me from her place.

I dreamed a terrible desire
  Came to my heart that was so cold
To feel again the old, dead fire
  And the dear thrill so old.

I dreamed—ah, then I woke to know
  The living ache, the long-sore smart
Had never gone from me, and oh,
  To know it smoothed my heart.

# THEN WOULD I DEEM MY SONG AND SINGING WELL.

If I could only sing a little song,
    Bearing no message deep or marvelous,
But breathing love and heart's-ease, or the long
    Sad nights when death has come to sit by us—
If lips but trembled while the dim eye read,
    Or parted, smiling, when the cadence fell,
Then I would deem my labour comforted;
    Then would I deem my song and singing well.

If I could only voice a little hope,
    A little way out of the dark despair,
Tho' it be found through tears, with hands that
        grope,
    For hearts gone lonely for lost lips and hair—
If some one sometimes laid my verse away
    (Oh, very seldom!) just to overspell,
When the mood comes—ah, that were richest pay!
    Then would I deem my song and singing well.

# THE SINGING WIRE.

# THREE AND TWO.

## I.

Once, hand to hand held low,
  With a little head between,
Under the blue of summer days,
We two went strolling thro' the ways
  When all the paths were green.

Ah, hand in hand, and slow,
  And reft of our delight,
Under the chill of wintry days,
We two went stumbling thro' the ways
  When all the paths were white.

# AH, CRUEL, SO CRUEL.

## II.

Deep eyes—so deep,
  Wide eyes, so winsome bright.
Red lips—so red,
  To strike mine own so white!
Ah, cruel, so cruel, to smile on mine which weep,
  Deep eyes—so deep!

Red lips—so red,
  Full lips so parted sweet.
Deep eyes—so deep,
  My wavering ones to meet!
Ah, cruel, so cruel, to laugh above my dead,
  Red lips—so red!

# STRAYED.

## III.

I took the road to Arcadie
   Within the realm of May,
And left my sweet with eager feet—
   Alas and welaway!
I took the road to Arcadie;
Dark grew the meadows and the sea;
Dull the fair sky seemed to me,
      And grey.

I turned my back on Arcadie
   All upon a day,
And with lagging feet, to find my sweet,
   Went back along the way.
Brighter the meadows grew and sea;
And then—I knew that aye to me,
Home with her was Arcadie
      And May.

# WHEN LOVE WITH THEE.

## IV.

When Love with thee
   To dwell his time is come,
Let him no memories see,
   Let other days be dumb.
Glad shouldst thou be
   So to forget awhile,
      And smile!

When Love goes by
   And passes in the gloom,
Set up no image high
   To sanctify his room.
So mayst thou sigh
   No longer than is best,
      And rest!

# THE LOVER.

## V.

She I love is white as milk.
  She I love is red as wine.
And her cheek is like spun-silk
  And her heart is mine.

When she runs, the rushes slip.
  When she stays, the lilies stir.
When she walks, the swallows dip,
  Keeping pace with her.

She I love is gold and fire.
  She I love is fruit in snow.
And her voice is silver wire,
  Touched with flaxen bow.

When she speaks, the fir-trees hush
  From their whispering on the hill.
When she sings, the very thrush
  For my sake is still.

# HIDE!

## VI.

Little white flower
  I scarce can discover—
Little white moth
  O'er blossoms a-hover,
      (Hide!)
Ne'er can I hide
  From the eyes of my lover!

Little white stone
  'Neath grasses a-quiver—
Little white moon
  With cloud passing over,
      (Hide!)
Ne'er would I hide
  From the lips of my lover!

Little white bird,
  Oh, pale little rover—
Little white wing
  In copse-woven cover,
      (Hide!)
Ne'er will I hide
  From the heart of my lover!

# REMEMBRANCE.

## VII.

Those lampless, loveliest eyes
      (O, smile!)
That follow me all the way.
Sweet eyes, wondering all the while
    As eyes that wander may.
Eyes so hungering and pale-browed—
Eyes that draw me out of the crowd—
      (O, smile!)

Those tenderest, wisest eyes
      (O, tears!)
That beckon me from the press.
Sad eyes, lingering all the years,
    Looking from loneliness.
Eyes wherein no drops can start—
Eyes that burn in my empty heart—
      (O, tears!)

NOCTURNE.

## VIII.

Crimson roses flaunt and flush
    Where her little feet are still,
  (She will know me when I come!)
  Where the homing beetle's hum
Only wakes the thrush.

    Clouds float over field and hill
Where her little hands are crossed;
  She will hear my footsteps pass
  (Underneath the burnished grass)
    As the lilies will.

Birds pipe in the alders, mossed
    Where her little heart is cold.
  (She will smile to know my tread
  Up above her golden head,
Thinking I was lost.)

    Where her loving heart is cold—
  Where her dancing feet are still—
Where her hands lie on her breast,
She is waiting in her rest.
    Tread not overbold.

# LINNET.

## IX.

Linnet and ruby-throat,
Less sweet your mellow note
   Than singing voice I know!
Swell all your feathered coat,
   Ne'er could your piping go
   Where she lies silent so.

Trill, shake and pulsing breast,
Give of your song the best;
   Hers was more full and fine.
Now she has stopped to rest
   Under the meadow vine.
   Poor little bird of mine!

# AS NONE BUT SHE COULD KNOW.

## X.

When the woods were keeping
  A leafy murmur low,
At thought of her a-sleeping
  Where lilies bend and blow
At thought of her a-sleeping,
Oh, I fell a-weeping
  As none but she could know.

For, when the snows are heaping
  And cold the winds must blow,
I thought of her a-sleeping
  With lilies all laid low—
I thought of her a-sleeping,
And oh, I fell a-weeping
  As none but she could know.

# A MANY YEARS AGO.

## XI.

I reached and broke a budding spray
And laid it on your lips that day—
Ah, dear, 'twas in that other May,
   A many years ago.
I kissed your lips and laid it there,
And, kissing, wound it with your hair,
   And laughed to see you so.

I reached and broke a budding spray
And laid it on your grave to-day,
And thought upon that other May,
   A many years ago.
And, dear, I kissed it with a smile,
And, kissing, lay a little while,
   Content to feel it so.

# THE WHITE LADY.

## XII.

(A little cry in the night,
  A little cloud in the gale.)
Your eyes—your eyes are bright
  And your cheek is pale.

My cheek—my cheek is wan
  Because my heart is cold.
The fields the sun gleams on,
  But my earth is old.

(A little cloud in the wind,
  A little sob in the dark.)
Oh, to my soul that sinned,
  Can you never hark?

Love that's lost in the gale!
  Grief that the silence hears!
Now but a cheek that's pale,
  And your wasted tears.

## XIII.

Old love is best,
Tho' pale with love's disdain.
Old love is best,
Tho' mixed of pride and pain.
Bid no new guest!
Old love is loveliest.

Old love is best,
Tho' new love promise more.
Old love is best,
Tho' flouted o'er and o'er.
Go back and rest!
Old love is tenderest.

# A SONG OF LOVE AND DUST.

## XIV.

Purple flower and soaring lark,
   Burnished wing and stamen's gold—
All must pass into the dark,
   Droop and mingle with the mould.
So, while yet your face I see,
   Bend and touch me; Sweet, kiss me.

Throbbing song and story brave,
   Holpen out with harp and tongue,
Silent are, where, in the grave
   Merry measure ne'er is sung.
So, while singing still may be,
   Bend and clasp me; Sweet, kiss me.

True love, lonely heart a-rust,
   Reddened cheek and joyless eye—
All must fall and come to dust,
   In the narrow house must lie.
So, while lovers now are we,
   Bend and fold me; Sweet, kiss me.

# PASSING.

## XV.

The sweetest song I sing
  Is for you, my dear.
Take it, all unwondering—
  Only yours to hear.

The fairest flower I meet—
  Just for you to hold.
Take it, though beneath your feet
  Other flowers are old.

I will not sing again.
  List the song to-day.
Smell its perfume once, and then
  Throw the flower away.

# HARMONICS.

# DAWN.

I dreamed I walked the forest and the woods were
    ablaze
    With smoky glory of autumn; the hills glowed
      light,
    And I dreamed she I loved came in a dress of
      white.
Pale and blown was her hair, as in old, lost days.

Weary were her eyes, and her round, white breast
    Rose and fell with her breath—swelled and died
      with her sigh,
    And she cried, " Oh, my love, come and kiss me
      where I lie!
Smooth, smooth my heart!  Dear love that hath
    my rest! "

Then the trees shook and drooped and the copse
    blazed red.
    I woke, weeping loud, and my love fled away,
    Trembling, starting and crying, and the dim,
      bare day
And the touch of the dawn lay cold on my head.

# NIGHT.

White face, loose hair, sighs and the fair, young
   breast—
What matter what star purples in the west?
Night dies, day wakes, but love—ah, love was best.

Quick heart, soft lips, love and the sweet, long kiss.
What matter what day offereth after this?
Morn breaks, noon pales, eve wanes, and then
   night is.

# SPUME OF THE SEA.

White shines the sand where the wavelets lap the
    shingle;
  Blow the breezes round about, burns the sunny
    noon;
Cold breaks the surf till the bathers' fingers tingle,
  Where at eve the lovers watch the white-faced
    moon.
Dear heart, sweet heart, come again and linger;
  Sand, sea and sun kiss away your hue of snow;
Where the needled pine becks with crook'd and
    lifted finger,
  Little one of old-time, thither let us go.

I will leave the gnawing pain, the soul-consuming
    sorrow,
  Cover up the tender hurt, put away the tears;
Just while we stay let the future own to-morrow:
  Let us love again as in the far fled years.
Dear heart, sweet heart, stilled your heart of throb-
    bing;
  Sand, sea and sun cannot clasp you where you lie.
Only I, with empty arms, empty heart, and sobbing,
  Wander lone and dreaming of the long gone by.

# VARIATION.

She whom I gave my furthest thought for proving
Could not  keep home her  little heart from roving,
So I called back my soul from her and grieving.

Slow time made on—then she, the old paths leav-
    ing,
Came seeking me, so slow and tiredly moving,
To have my love that died for want of having.

So found she careless me, her fair breast heaving;
Showed me  her heart  and called it worth the  sav-
    ing—
Me—in whose heart lay buried love and loving!

## MELODIC.

Dear, when my eyes told the age-old story,
    Tongue-tied, faltering, breath quick drawn,
Say, did you see where a crimson-tinted glory,
    Star-shot, trembled to a new day's dawn?

Dear—but I saw it!   And the rich light, leaning,
    Moon-hung, marvelous, warmed by breeze,
Gave to the dim dusk a new and vibrant meaning,
    World wide, scented with the soul's heart's-ease.

Dear, then my lips knew no need of any telling!
    Dear, then, trembling, caught I up my crown!
For, by that overglow, my own love's dwelling
    Saw I, lying in your heart deep down.

# THERE IS A GRAVE.

There is a grave where some one sleeps—
Some one sleeps whom some one weeps.
  Still, so still you cannot hear one,
  Ne'er can hear one calling, dear one,
    Calling o'er and o'er.

In this grave where some one lies—
Some one lies whom some one's sighs
  Cover warm—you cannot greet one,
  Ne'er can greet one calling, sweet one,
    Ne'er can hear me more!

# COMES SHE.

Sweet my love and fleet my love, and runs my love
  to kiss me?
Roams she o'er the misty moor, lists she on the lea?
Comes she down with springing step and open arms
  that miss me?
Feathered rush and little rill, how comes she?

Oh my love and dear my love, and walks my love
  to meet me?
Stands she at the heather's edge harkening for me?
Waits she with a heavy heart and aching arms to
  greet me?
Tufted cloud and little wind, how comes she?

Sweet my love and dear my love, or glad or sad she
  find me,
Speeds she swift or lags she slow—so she come to
  me—
Comes she with her love alone and both her arms
  to bind me.
Leaning heart and little hands—so comes she.

# IN THE RAIN.

Only just a year ago,
  Thro' the summer weather,
We two wandered slow
  Down the paths together.

    Sun's kiss, rain's kiss,
      Why is it, I wonder?
    I here, and you there,
      The green grass under.

Only just a year ago?
  No, but ah, it seems so!
Years stretch wide, and oh,
  Loneliness will dream so!

    Sun's kiss, rain's caress;
      Only I to wander,
    With my heart by your heart,
      Lying over yonder.

# SOMEWHERE.

Somewhere—somewhere safe from the cold,
  Waits my little one, somewhere.
Waits, while the weary years grow old,
Wanting my lips and my love to fold—
  Wanting, though pain is dumb there,
  Waits my little one, somewhere.

Somewhere—somewhere safe from the heat,
  Waits my little one, somewhere.
Not with dead lilies at head and feet
(But oh, what we laid there was so sweet!)
  And after awhile I shall come where
  Waits my little one, somewhere.

Weary days and dreary days, and what is it you
bring me?
Only toil that I have known? Tell me, is it all?
Bring you not an evensong that my tired heart can
sing me—
A song to light the shadows in the cold night
fall?

Dreaming days and seeming days, and what is it
you tell me?
Hide you hope to follow this? Hold you joy to
be?
Know you not a tender charm that memory shall
spell me—
A charm to fright the sorrows that await lone
me?

Olden days and golden days, I know the price you
pay me.
Never more can I rise up to those ripe days that
were.
Give me only in the dark a little prayer to pray me—
A prayer to pray when I lie down, now night
holds her!

# LOST.

Knew I the day when the bird piped
   And the stream ran wild and free,
And the wind sang by and the cloud sailed high,
   As sweet as sweet could be.
Now the dark has fallen on the meadow
   And the mist has risen from the sea,
And the bird and the stream and the wind and the
     cloud
   Go seeking, seeking me.

Knew I the day of a song, dear,
   And a smile that was its key,
And a love so white and a kiss so light,
   And I held them all in fee.
Now the world is lost in the shadow
   And I am old, maybe,
And the song and the smile and the love and the
     kiss
   Go seeking, seeking me.

## SPRING'S KISS.

Sweet one, little one, warm one—see.
Look where the apple-blooms fall near me.
Soft, soft, soft as the first white snows,
Covering the mound where no green grass grows.

Sweet one, little one, dear one—see.
(Think I how bitter apple-bloom may be!)
Soft, soft, soft, with a lisping stir,
Meet to lie so near above that smile of her.

# THE CALLING WINDS.

Weariness and heart-ache, and longing that is
 lonely—
 A sobbing in the little winds that blow around
 the door;
Eyes' mist and dropping tears, and all my life is
 only
 A sighing in a darkened house, a shadow on the
 floor.

Emptiness and unrest, and waiting that is weary—
 A crying in the little leaves that crisp upon the
 plain;
Hope's dust and love's despair, and—oh, my van-
 ished dearie!
 My heart is on the night wind, my soul is in
 the rain!

# REQUIEM.

Saddened the laggard day;
   Flags fluttered low.
Grieving the waterway;
   Ships trailing slow.
Gone are the bitter days;
   Low—low his head.
Only the victor's bays
   For the great dead.

    Blow, breezes;
    Ripple, river;
  Flame, western sun.
So be soldiers' quiet slumber
   When battle's done!

Silent the leaden song
   When war shall cease.
Dead be the bitter wrong,
   Buried in peace.

Over a shaken land,
  Slow, slow the years.
After the iron hand,
  Love—love and tears.

    Blow, breezes;
    Ripple, river;
  Sun, gild the West.
So be heroes' quiet slumber.
  God holds the rest!

## MOODS.

When I walked in the sunshine, singing
   Of hopes that were blithe and free,
Came Love with his round arms clinging,
   And the warmth of his kiss warmed me.

When I sat in the night heavy-hearted,
   With fears that were dull and dree,
Then love hid his face and departed
   And the chill of the dark chilled me.

# HEART'S URN.

Ah, me! the rosied hours were fleet
   In that sweet time!
Our hearts sang on with every beat
   Love's old, worn rhyme.
To little feet our steps were slow,
   The bells were all in chime—
And this is why I sorrow so
   In this sad time.

Ah, me! no more the days are sweet
   As that sweet day!
No more I hear the dancing feet
   Of her child play.
No more I hold the hands I love,
   No more my song is gay—
Oh, what my heart holds ashes of
   On this sad day!

L. of C.

# THE PHILOSOPHER AND THE WORLD.

Life is toil
　　And its days drag dreary.
When Death comes,
　　It finds us weary;
Glad to lie
　　With our limbs laid straitly,
Eyes fast shut
　　That were tired so lately;
Flesh and its fleetness
　　Under sod;
Soul's meek meetness
　　Gone to God.

Life is toil
　　And its days drag dreary.
But ah, toil's sweet
　　When your eyes shine, dearie.
Tired am I
　　At the day's dusk closes,
Tired—but to rest
　　In your red love's roses.
Were I only
　　Under sod,
I should be lonely
　　Up with God.

# THREE SONNETS.

Let her but love me, Lord, and loving, stay
  Near, ever nearer where my bare heart is,
  Deeming at length that naught can count save
    this—
The touch of loved lips' meeting in love's May.
So shall my bitterness pass quite away,
  And I, who have done many things amiss,
  Shall feel Thy lovingkindness in her kiss,
And, knowing heaven here, shall learn to pray.

Let this but be for me!   Lord, I will hark
  To her soul's whispers, guide her slender feet,
  Hold up her hands and fold her at the last,
  When, for our rest, life's little leagues are
    passed,
  And, looking further, skies shall ope more sweet,
While the dead world sinks into dreaming dark.

## II.

"God's Child" we called her, knowing not if He
  Had shaped her frailly to require her soon
    (So delicate-sweet she seemed for life's bluff
      dune
Putting on grace like a pale, little tree);
And when she passed, through girlish May, to be
  Rarer, more womanly from noon to noon,
    "God's Child" we called her still.  So her ripe
      June
Looked level love from her deep eyes to me.

God's Child!  May she lie ever in His sight,
  Folded and guarded by His loving smile.
    Only—the while she loves this Earth of
      Thine,
Give me to hold and comfort as I might.
  Let me look to her, God, this little while!
    Let me but dream Thy little child is mine!

# III.

If Night should take you from me, little one,
   And the grave's ice should turn your red to grey,
   While I, unsummoned, lonely, still must stay
Within the faded summer and sad sun—
I would not long to die, but, just begun,
   I would live out my love. I would not pray
   Forgetfulness, but light each difficult day
Remembering all the dear days that were done.

If it were well, you would be near me yet.
   If ill—if I could never, never touch
      Your soul with fire—if love dies with the
      breath,
Why—till my full fate's stars were sunk and set,
   I'd hug my little hope and, glorying much,
      Would cheat the dearest pang of coming death !

# WHITE-CLOVER.

# THE PRAYERS THE LITTLE CHILDREN SAY.

The prayers the little children say—
  They are not fine of speech,
But they hold deeper mystery
  Than any tome could teach,
And they reach further up to heaven
  Than wiser prayers can reach.
The angels laugh to hear each day
The prayers the little children say.

The prayers the little children say
  No toiling angel brings.
They pass right through the shining ray
  That searches selfish things.
(They are so little that they slip
  Between the guarding wings.)
And God says, "Hush and give them way!"
The prayers the little children say.

The prayers the little children say—
  Ah, if we knew the same!
For ours, so wise and gaunt and grey,
  Walk wearily and lame,
And by the time they come to God
  They have forgot his name.
Would we may sometime learn to pray
The prayers the little children say!

# AT PLAY.

The children play in the fields,
  And I who watch am a man,
Knowing the struggle and strife and toil
  With work and a hope and a plan;
Bowing my knee to the rod
  The King of my Leisure wields.
But my heart—my heart is ever at play
  With the children in the fields.

My heart is ever at play,
  Ever at play in the fields,
Smelling the perfume windy-sweet
  The clover blossom yields;
Smiling with curious gaze
  At its elders over the way,
And harking back to the green again,
  Where my heart is ever **at play.**

# LITTLE ALFIE INGLES.

To-day there crept into my ears
　　Some note of children's playing
That brought a thrill of buried years
　　Which frost is overlaying.
Again I smelled the fields in May,
　　And felt the winter's tingles
In swamp and wood, in school and play,
　　With little Alfie Ingles.


The years lie thick and deep since then,
　　For time can tarry never,
And most of us are bearded men
　　While some are children ever.
You went before my heart grew cold
　　With all the snows life mingles,
You missed the pain of growing old—
　　Dear little Alfie Ingles.


The dusk is falling as I dream—
　　The dusk of memory's closes,

And these faint scents of childhood seem
  The dust of long-dead roses.
A little stone, grass-grown in fall—
  These jarring little jingles—
My pipe-smoke and my thoughts are all.
  Oh, little Alfie Ingles!

# THE MASTER.

When my ship comes in—
   Oh, I shall be a-watching.
I shall stand upon the cliff and laugh for very joy.
   The form upon her deck
     Will be one that I remember;
It will look as I looked, when I was a boy.

When my ship comes in—
   Oh, I shall know her Captain.
He will wear the look I wore when I was clean
     and young.
   He will raise his hand
     With a gesture I remember,
When from out the halyards the signal flags are
     flung.

When my ship comes in—
   Oh, but I am dreaming!
The boy that watches on the cliff never a-land may
     be.
   Long, long since she put out,
     (It's oh, but I remember!)
'Tis I who am her Captain, and we labour far at sea.

# PRESENTIMENT.

"Now I lay me down to sleep"—
    (Twilight and a mother's knee)
Drooping head and fast-shut eyes,
Tender hands held praying-wise;
    Come the low words lispingly.
(Grey dusk falling dim and deep)
'Now I lay me down to sleep."

"Pray the Lord my soul to keep"—
    (Loving ear leaned down to list)
Sinless, stainless, day by day,
Has so white soul need to pray
    Whom the angels must have kist?
(Far the fingered shadows creep)
"Pray the Lord my soul to keep."

"If I die before I wake"—
    (Lips that part in sudden fright)
Ah, dear Lord! could eyes so dear
Close forever on us here?
    God! If it should be to-night!

(Heaving breast and hands that shake)
" If I die before I wake."


" Pray the Lord my soul to take."
      (Stifled cry and sobbing breath)
Kisses fierce as for the dead,
Tears upon the yellow head.
      " Let this shadow pass ! " she saith.
(Heart, poor heart, that soon must ache)
" Pray the Lord my soul to take."

# LAMP-LIGHT.

Dear little lady, so tumbled and sleepy,
    Kneeling at dusk with her head on my knee!
Lamp-light is dim and the shadows are creepy,
    Dear little lady, and ah, sad me!

Saying a prayer that the angels must soften—
    Ah, little lady, could only it be!—
Time was when I prayed too, often and often,
    Longing for one that we ne'er shall see.

Dear little lady, till play-days are over,
    Kneel here at dusk at my own tired knee.
How could you know what is under the clover?
    Dear little lady, but ah, sad me!

# THE YEARS OF OUR LIVES.

Our hearts are cold, our eyes are dry,
   And have been many a day.
How very seldom now we weep;
   How very seldom pray!

We know no vision's mystery;
   We washed our eyes for sight;
We sold, for hard, white, empty day,
   Our happy dreams at night.

The loves, the sorrows of child-time,
   The tears, so passing brief,
Are set to passion's deeper rhyme
   And a profounder grief.

We hear the children at their play—
   Their " Lay me down to sleep ";
We'd barter all life's laughs away
   If, like them, we could weep. ·

Our hearts are cold, our eyes are dry,
   And have been many a day.
How very seldom now we weep;
   How very seldom pray!

# GOLDY-LOCKS.

Oh pretty little goldy-locks
   I loved when age was callow,
With rundown shoes and tomboy frocks,
   Pink-stained with wild musk mallow,
And corn that stood in yellow shocks
To make our playhouse, goldy-locks.

Oh tumbled, little goldy-locks
   Who whistled to my hallo
In days of flag and four o'clocks
   And pumpkins lit with tallow,
Where 'neath the crimson hollyhocks
We grew together, goldy-locks.

Oh sweetheart, little goldy-locks,
   Life's deep seas then were shallow;
They knew no shipwreck, hid no rocks
   Life's lands were fair and fallow.
Oft at my heart sweet memory knocks,
Oh little, dear, dead goldy-locks!

# IN THE SHADOW.

I and she alone together,
  Only we two in the red lamp's glow.
Drear on the pane sobs the weary weather—
  Somehow it strains my throat cords so.

There are some toys in a wicker basket,
  High on a shelf that is all their own.
Deep as I look in the dark and ask, it
  Never will tell why we sit alone.

I and she, but our hands are colder—
  Paler her face in the red lamp's glow.
Maybe we just are growing older,
  Only—somehow—I remember so!

# LITTLE JEANNIE LUNDY.

I had a little sweetheart once,
  When boyhood's days were fleeting,
Who ate my apples, called me dunce,
  And smiled at me in meeting.
I lagged at school to see her go, and welcomed
    every Monday,
Because it brought the task again and—little
    Jeannie Lundy.


Dear childhood! And sweet youthful rhyme!
  What tunes its measures carried!
Ah, little playmates of that time,
  Now long grown up and married!
She married Frank, the baker's son—we fought
    each other one day;
Now plump and matronly, I know, is little Jean-
    nie Lundy.


Long years have flown and thin and grey
  The thatch my years are bringing;

But, even yet, a sunny day—
   A bird-note, or the singing
When I sit in my family pew—I sometimes do!
   on Sunday,
Brings back a thought of childhood's days an
   little Jeannie Lundy.

# THE LINGERING KISS.

That day I came upon a letter lying
　　In some forgotten nook, and oh, to see,
My ears seemed listening to a distant crying
　　That not for long and long had been for me.

I opened it and conned it o'er and o'er,
　　Quivering to ghostly fingers long forgot
That groped upon my heart to find a sore
　　In some long hidden yet familiar spot.

I thought on olden dreams now long decaying—
　　Ah me! That buried things can stir at all!
And then—I heard a shout of children playing,
　　And little footsteps pattering up the hall.

I laid the letter back to lie unseen,
　　And tried to think whatever is is best.
And then a sunny head came in between
　　Myself and that old soreness in my breast.

But there were tears upon my cheek, and stronger
　　Was something rising in my throat, I know,
And on the golden hair my kiss lay longer
　　That night.　We women cherish memories so!

# LITTLE BO-PEEP.

Little Bo-Peep sits on my knee—
    Little Bo-Peep with head of gold,
Softly singing in baby key
    Of a poor little sheep that was out in the cold;
    A poor little sheep that had lost its fold,
Just that a sad little song might be
    For little Bo-Peep with her three years old
To sit and solemnly sing to me.

Ready for bed is little Bo-Peep
    As she sits and sings while I hold her tight;
Her serious eyes are round and deep,
    Her little night-gown is soft and white.
    And she sings of the sheep that was lost in the
      night,
Lost in the cold while her lambkins weep
    Till the words grow sleepy, the eyes shut tight
And little Bo-Peep is fast asleep.

Little Bo-Peep sleeps on my knee—
    Little Bo-Peep with her three years old—

While I think of the song in that baby key
   Of the poor little sheep that is out in the cold;
   My poor little sheep that has lost its fold,
Out in the storm and the dark, maybe,
   While little Bo-Peep, with her head of gold,
Sits and solemnly sings to me.

# THE MESSENGERS.

The little children, in whose eyes
    Young faith is deep and clear,
Gaze on the world with shy surprise,
    With laughter light and dear.
They guess not evil is so wise
    And grief than smiles more near.

They know but joy.   Their souls are white,
    Their little hearts are soft.
They dream of heaven in the night,
    They pray and wonder oft.
For their own innocence hath might
    To lift them up aloft.

Last night—I dreamed I was a child.
    I dropped my weary years.
I felt the mother-fingers mild,
    That soothed my childish fears.
And when I woke, with longing wild,
    My face was wet with tears.

# UNCOMFORTED.

The gates of pearl and chrysoprase
  Stand gleaming in the sun—
Oh, I can see his wondering gaze,
  My little quiet one!

Heaven is wide, its ways are sweet
  For souls grown wise and bold,
But all too soft are baby feet
  To tire on streets of gold.

His holy Throne—the shining Band—
  His Angels bowing near—
Oh, Mary, take him by the hand,
  If I must tarry here!

My cheek is softer than a crown,
  And sweeter was the rest
Of baby eyes my hand pressed down
  To sleep against my breast.

Than twice ten thousand cherubim
    All jubilant of tongue,
Oh, tenderer was the cradle hymn
    That my low lips have sung.

His little hands—his feet so white—
    His lips that warmed my own—
Oh, Mary, make his bed to-night
    Lest he should feel alone!

# LITTLE BOY BLUE.

### (E. F.)

The little toy dog that was covered with dust
And the little tin soldier, red with rust,
Came dancing down, with a skip and a hop,
From the high top-shelf of the toy-seller's shop
To sit in the window, full in view,
And wait for the coming of Little Boy Blue.

"We heard—oh, we heard," they softly sighed,
"That the Little Boy Blue of ours had died."
"There's a little grey book on the shelf, I know,"
Said the little toy dog, "and it told me so!"
Then the little tin soldier shook his head.
"Just as if rhymes were true!" he said.

But the old toy-seller he set them by
With a wavering tear in his dim, old eye,
Till some one came with a skip and a hop
To bear them away from the dark old shop—
And they laughed to think it was Little Boy Blue,
But he knew that the little rhyme-book said true.

# LAVENDER.

Of all things fond and treasured here,
  Far dearest are, I know, to her
The little garments that my dear
  Has laid away in lavender.

She folded them so long ago—
  I quite forget how many years—
Smoothing them down with fingers slow
  That could not find their way for tears.

I know she kissed them one by one,
  And patted them, just as she did
So often, after day was done,
  The little blue-check coverlid.

I never look at them, for men—
  God knows my heart is bitter yet!
But she—will steal away, and then
  Go silent, with her lashes wet.

Such times I know that she has knelt,
  For a long hour, sad-sweet to her,
In some dim, silent nook that smelt
  Of buried things and lavender.

We never speak, you know, of this;
  It must not seem less far away,
But when, some nights, I feel her kiss—
  Sometimes—I do not dare to pray!

# THE MOTHER.

A little ring of gold—a battered shoe—
    A faded, curling wisp of yellow hair—
Some penciled pictures—playthings one or two—
    A corner and a chest to hold them there.

Many a woman's fondest hoard is this,
    Among her dearest treasures none so dear,
Though bearded lips are often hers to kiss
    That once made only prattle to her ear.

The sturdy arm, the seasoned form, the brow
    That arches over eyes of manly blue
Mean all joy to her living memory now,
    And yet—and yet—she hugs the other too!

With that rare love, mysterious and deep,
    Down in a mother-heart thro' all the years,
That placid age can never lull to sleep
    And is not grief, yet oft brings foolish tears,

She often goes those hoarded things to view
    And finger the wee treasures hidden there—
To touch the little ring and battered shoe
    And kiss the curling wisp of yellow hair.

# ONLY A LAUGH.

Only a laugh, but the joy of the hours in it,
　　Dropping so blithely from out of the gloom,
Down from the casement that has the red flowers
　　　　in it,
　　Flooding with sunshine my poor little room.

Only a laugh—but I know well whose choice it is.
　　Oh, I can guess whose the lips that can chaff,
Whose is the smiling mouth, whose bubbling voice
　　　　it is,
　　Putting such perfume in only a laugh.

Only a laugh!　My lone life is so shadowy,
　　Tinged with the darkness that solitude grows,
Most of the brightness missed, most of its glad
　　　　away,
　　Most of its tenderness chilled by the snows.

Only a laugh, but so much of the gay in it!
　　Oh, were there love, 'twould be sweeter by half.
I could forget that my hair has its grey in it
　　Were it for me more than—only a laugh!

## MUTE WITNESSES.

The soft lamp gilds my desk to-night;
    My books stand all a-row.
I turn them o'er, and to my sight
    They seem to sorrow so!

The ancient rhymes of love and death
    That were such comforters
Seem now to know some living breath
    That all about them stirs.

Story and fable, quaint and good,
    They speak so bitterly!
Not as the hand that penned them would
    That they should speak to me.

A little comment scribbled fine.
    A finger-print, a bit
Of folded paper at some line
    Tells how we talked of it.

Alike the poet and the sage,
  Gold-edge and russet-brown—
A penciled word upon a page,
  A corner folded down!

The glamour of **the** verse is flown;
  The cut leaves seem to bleed.
In the dim light I read alone
  The books she loved to read.

# FOR ALL THESE THINGS.

I thank Thee, Lord, for wind and snow,
For the brown wren upon the bough.
   I thank Thee for the level rain,
   For the grey cloud and wrinkled plain,
For running water and bright grass,
For eyesight that all this joy has.
   And, most of all, I thank Thee for
   The thankfulness I have in store.

I thank Thee, Lord, for work and rest,
For all glad dreams within my breast.
   I thank Thee for the way I win,
   For my chid faults and early sin,
For childhood, kisses and the sky,
For chance to live and hope to die.
   And, most of all, I thank Thee for
   This want of mine to thank Thee more.

# PASTELLES.

# THREE THINGS.

Three things there be that are all sweet,
Sweetest of all things vanishing
And dearest, dearest far of all:

A child's kiss, stumbling so and fleet,
Straight-falling rain of later spring,
Loved footsteps coming up a hall.

# BESTOWAL.

Kiss me!
I nevermore shall weep again.
Sorrow will pass me like the passing rain.
Old griefs must seem so little and so far—
Not meet for lips whereon such chaplets are!

Kiss me!
I nevermore shall laugh again.
Past joys grow poor and meaningless as pain;
All dear delights I knew so little blest—
Not fit to lie whereon such roses rest!

# THE PAGAN.

And her god shall be her husband.—*Kama Soutra.*

I pay no fee to sanctity,
   For priestly praise or blame;
The little leaves within the wood
   Through which my dearest came—
The little leaves within the wood
   Are covered with his name.

I take no heed to templed rede,
   Of holy wine or meat;
The little pebbles on the way
   Where went my master sweet—
The little pebbles on the way
   Are singing of his feet.

# THE PERVERSE.

Silently I sit,
 Soberly I walk.
All the tenderness of it
 Banished from her talk!

Could I jest or sing,
 Or forget awhile—
Could I tell her anything
 That would bring her smile!

It was murder red,
 It was murder white,
Those few bitter words I said
 On that bitter night!

'Twas a devil lay
 Curled within my soul.
I would give my life away,
 To take back the whole!

It is mine to weep,
 It is mine to bow,
But the devil in me deep,
 Will not let me now.

# THE MASK.

Watch her if she turn
  Hitherway her head.
Guess you on those calm lips burn
  Kisses that are dead?

All the fond and sweet
  Vanished from her brow.
Tremulous and very fleet
  Is her smiling now!

Only just a year
  Gulfs the now and then—
It were better if a tear
  Lash her eye again.

It were better much
  If she rocked and wept,
If she trembled to a touch
  Of the love that slept!

This is woman's art—
  So serene and proud;
Would you guess her very heart
  Is sobbing out aloud?

# THE THRESHOLD.

I shall wait for you where I stand
 Looking into the opening view,
Unless you have gone to the selfsame land,
 And there is only a step to you.

You might be tempted to stray from me,
 To follow the little face we missed.
But I would linger—ah, wait and see!
 Knowing him somewhere warm and kissed.

So I shall pray to go over first
 (If God will listen and let it be),
And then the newness of it will burst
 On us both together, you and me.

# REQUIESCAT.

When our little day is done,
 When our tinsel sun is set,
When the long night is begun,
 Where our waking stars are met,

Thinking not on how we fell,
 Error wide or failure deep—
Let us dream it all was well,
 Let us smile and so to sleep.

Wondering, mayhap, at the blot
 Death has dropped to end the play,
Marveling that our hearts were hot
 Or beat fiercely yesterday.

# ROCOCO.

# EPITAPH.

Out of the dead man's breast
Orchids sprouted richly dressed;

Out of the dead man's eyes,
Pansies purple as evening's skies.

But out of his heart no flower had grown,
For his heart was naught but a rounded stone.

# THE TWINS.

One was slender and white of blee—
   The clock strikes one—the clock strikes one!—
And one was dark, though fair to see,
   And I sit on in the dark.

A lover one had in a far countree—
   The stroke is done—the stroke is done!—
Oh, that she now his bride might be,
   While I sit on in the dark.

I loved that lover, ah, woe is me!
   For I had none—for I had none!—
For I was the other, as you see,
   As I sit on in the dark.

The lover came back from over the sea—
   In storm and sun—in storm and sun!—
But he found the fair one dead at my knee,
   And I sit on in the dark.

He mourned her long, he weeps her free—
   I was the one—I was the one!—
And he gave not even his curses to me,
   So I sit on in the dark.

# VILLANELLE.

She is the bitter and the sweet.
　　She is the pleasure and the pain—
My thorned flowers springing 'round her feet!

For love her lips are curved and meet.
　　For hate her brows are straight and plain.
She is the bitter and the sweet.

Dawn the days ever, slow or fleet.
　　I know life's sunshine and its rain—
My thorned flowers springing 'round her feet!

My prone self is her laughter's seat.
　　My proud soul is her incensed fane.
She is the bitter and the sweet.

She pierced my heart and stilled its beat;
　　Her tears made all her slaying vain—
My thorned flowers springing 'round her feet!

I lie warm in my winding-sheet,
　　By her twin kisses saved and slain.
She is the bitter and the sweet.
My thorned flowers springing 'round her feet.

# THE MAD MUSICIAN.

A harp would I—a harp whose touch,
  In sunlight, star-fire, glamoured dusk,
  Would prick my senses fine as musk,
Whose voice would charm me overmuch.

It must be strung all cunningly,
  Its cords fine-wove and music-mad,
  Like her dark hair that made me glad
To singing when I wound it free.

Its frame a marvel would I make,
  Fair-shaped and rounded as is best,
  Like the full curves that formed her breast
To thrill such cadence when she spake.

On harp deft-fashioned tone to tone,
  Ah me, what music would I dare!
  Whose strings were twist of her rich hair,
And its frame carved out of her breast-bone.

# THE MONK.

The monk went down the winding stair
  And lit the candles one by one.
The heavy incense in the air
  Made each a nimbused sun.

The corpse lay lighted on its bier;
  Its cheek was white, its eyes were dim,
But suddenly they opened clear
  And wavered up at him.

"Brother," it said—and well he knew
  That it was dead that spake so wise—
"Since yestere'en I have had view
  Of Heaven, with these eyes.

"The Radiance looked upon my face
  And on the holy dress I wore;
There was for me no heavenly place,
  For that my heart was sore.

" So thrust your hand within my breast
　　And take away my mortal sin,
That when I go once more to rest,
　　I may so enter in."


The monk drew wide the dead man's dress
　　And lo, a pictured face he bore.
It lay so light, so light, nathless
　　It made the dead heart sore.


Quick he unclasped the painted thing
　　As one of his own soul afraid,
And hurled it from him shuddering,
　　And shudderingly prayed.


The dead man sweated as he lay,
　　And a sharp trembling shook each limb;
But when the fit had passed away
　　The eyes smiled, and were dim.


The monk awoke (the bell that day
　　Tolled for the dead man o'er and o'er)
And knew, the while he tried to pray,
　　His own dead heart was sore.

# A DEAD MAN.

Set ye the candles burning near.
Know ye the death that is not to fear?
Take ye the saying, ye who hear—
   "Sleep, who sleep!
    Wake, who wake!
    But be as the dead
    For the dead man's sake."


Writ that one might read who ran,
There on his forehead, "I was a man."
Take ye the saying, ye who can—
   "Sleep, who sleep!
    Wake, who wake!
    But be as the dead
    For the dead man's sake."

# THE GLANCING ARROW.

They said, " The face that yesternight
Looked rosily, is now gone white.
Your neighbor sits across the street
With ashes on his head and feet."

I strode across with eyes undim,
Ungrieving, for I hated him.
I sped my joy on sorrow's wing
And thought to taunt in comforting.

I looked to hear his curse and see
His hate pierce my hypocrisy—
But she who loved him so lay warm
(And watching us) upon God's arm.

He saw, but grief had made him blind.
He heard, but, hearing, thought me kind.
I who had hated all the years,
Had saved his reason by his tears!

# THE BRIGHT, WISE SNAKE OF EDEN.

He said, "Her body is a clod."
  (Oh, fair as sight of heaven!)
He said, "'Tis wove of rain and sod.
What has love to do with God?
  (The bright, wise Snake of Eden.)
A shiver of wind in the dry beard-grass.
Never a love that will not pass!"

I drew my dear with my two eyes.
  (Oh, sweet as eyes in heaven!)
"Lilith loved thee tender-wise
Or ever she walked in woman guise.
  (The bright, wise Snake of Eden.)
Or ever in Adam's arm she lay
Ere Adam loved a woman of clay."

I showed him my heart of blue and red.
  (Oh, fond as love in heaven!)
My love lay there like a flower that bled;
My breast was healed by the words she said.
  (The bright, wise Snake of Eden.)

I showed him my soul of purpled light.
My love lay there like a flower of white.

I couched my dear upon my breast.
　(Oh, dear as God in heaven!)
And kissed her eyelids down to rest
Till she slept soundly, as was best.
　(The bright, wise Snake of Eden.)
I said, " As Lilith's love for thee,
As thine for Lilith, our love shall be ! "

He veiled his lidless eyes with grass.
　(Oh, cruel as death in heaven!)
He wept such tears as a woman has,
For the love of Lilith would not pass !
　(The bright, wise Snake of Eden.)
And I laughed, and my dear leaped, clinging wild—
Half-dreaming—like a frighted child.

# LOVE'S DEATH-IN-LIFE.

As I lay sleeping on my bed,
Love came and stood above my head.
He bent and kissed me as was meet;
I wound my hair about his feet.
But when I would not let him go,
He stabbed me deep my heart below.
My soul was clean and baby-wise
And God unfolded Paradise.

The women came by three and three
To sew a burial dress for me.
They washed my body with perfume
And set fine odours round the room.
They combed my hair—my poor delight,
And hid my heart with flowers of white.
My soul gave ear to all their sighs
Where it lay sick in Paradise.

But while my corse—may Christ me save!
Lay that night in new-made grave,

Love came and wrought my face to see,
And lay down in the grave with me.
The tears in his dear eyes gave light
That made my cerements gold-bright.
He kissed me thrice on cheek and eyes
And my soul hated Paradise.

# GALILEE.

When Jesus went walking on Galilee
Wide went the wonder on shore and sea.
The rowers bent out to the spent wind's call,
And, fearful, to other they answered all:
"Is it the Master who fares to us?
What should be message He bears to us?"
    And the ship, rocked rover,
    On cloud above her,
    Made sign of the cross
    With her mast bent over.

When Jesus went walking on Galilee,
The wind hid its face on the labouring sea.
The little waves plodded around His feet,
Calling out, each more wise and sweet:
"This is the Master who fares to them.
Let us listen the message He bears to them!"
    And the ship, rocked rover,
    On cloud above her,
    Made sign of the cross
    With her mast bent over.

# THE DEAD HEART.

Now I am dead and have no share
   In life (from living passed away)—
Now I no more may breathe the air,
   And all to-days are yesterday,

I do bethink me of a thing
   That, like a dusty memory, yet
Follows me herein wandering;
   Nor would I quite forget.

Within the hollow of my breast
   There lay a something, I recall,
Which, when I came into my rest,
   Throbbed nevermore at all.

A thing that fragrant was and rare;
   It stirred and throbbed and throbbing,
     sung—
Oh, it was fine and it was rare,
   And sweet it was and young!

So, it was pleasant thus to take
  My sleep at length and smell the rain,
And know no nerve might ever ache
  Or know the name of pain.

My dead world dulled herself apace—
  My bed was part and part of her—
Till being sifted on her face
  Its grains of things that were.

And then the naked, shivering *I*
  Rose up and smote itself and cried
For what it knew could never die
  And had not ever died.

'Twas in the hollow of my breast—
  Beneath its rounded arch it lay.
Now I have come into my rest
  And all to-days are yesterday.

# THE GARGOYLE.

I am a gargoyle gaunt and grey,
Carved in an ancient, ancient day,
    Aloft and alone
    On a coping of stone,
Chained far out of a mortal's way;
  Perched by the flange of a leaden gutter,
  Where the street roar dies to a mutter,
Lean of muzzle and lank of limb,
Gaunt and grey and jagged and grim.

Up to my air floats the belfry's tone,
When the cathedral chimes are flown,
    To be down-hurled
    To the skirt of the world—
And then I must bow to the notes alone!
  In and among them beats the shout
  Of sturdy watchman and roustabout,
Joyous, while I crouch still and drear,
Grizzled of mane and cold of ear.

Once—a workman crawled on high
And swung his ladder across my sky,
    Clinging, bold,
    To my claws' stone-hold,
And fondling me with his hands—and I—
  Would have bent him and flung him down—
    down—down—
  Onto the seething, human town,
Only—the chimes began just then,
And I had to bow me to God again!

# THE DARK BRIDAL.

Up to the sky flew a fiend one night
And whispered love to an angel white;
As heaven the angel's heart lay bare,
Ne'er had a passion slumbered there.
   "Love, love, love!" was the devil's hymn;
   "Sin, sin, sin!" sung the seraphim.
"Haste! O'er each glory-tinted head
Fold ye your shining wings," God said.

To the angel's lips sprang a first-born sob,
Into her heart crept a mortal throb;
Warm grew her fringed and purple eyes,
Cold stretched her bleak-walled Paradise.
   "Love, love, love!" sung the sin-song slow;
   "Sweet, sweet, sweet!" sighed the angel low.
(Bring bell and book and let prayers be said.
The angel goes to the devil's bed.)

# RECOGNITION.

## I.

Eyes I covered up with grass—
Smile you yet where I shall pass?

Hair I wound and unwound so,
Smelling it, smoothing it—are you so?

Nay, for the hair is dull and rust.
Nay, for the eyes are dim and dust.


## II.

Yet stay.   Oft when my lids closed down,
Hearing never a lisp of her gown,

Seeing not, smelling no scent of hers
(As I go now, 'neath this lonely curse)

Pressing nor hand nor touching hair—
Yet was I happy knowing her there.

## III.

Not lip, limb, eye or head of gold,
Not smile, tear, word, shall I see, hear, hold —

Not any of these but a nearer thing,
Rarer than her earth-fashioning.

This I shall feel, shall possess, shall know.
The I and She!   And the rest may go.

# THE LONG JOURNEY.

Never were dying eyes, I ween,
But gave to a meadow a lovelier green.
Ne'er is a death of what we see
But feeds a life in the is to be.
The bee builds comb and the bird its nest
'Neath the rifted roof of a dead man's breast.

What for thee in this dusty plan?
Ye with your mighty mind of man!
What are the bee and bird to thee?
Wait, and waiting ye may see!
Well it be, an ye be not guest
'Neath the rifted roof of a dead man's breast!

# ISOBEL.

*" Blessed is the bride that the sun shines on.*
*Blessed is the corpse that the rain rains on.*

Oh fairest the face that so fickle heart has won!
(Blessed is the bride that the sun shines on.)
    For her the ruddy lip and for her the lighted eye,
    Silver hasp and bridal clasp and robe laid by.
Oh soft cheek, tint of rose!  Oh snow-white
    breast of swan!
(Blessed is the bride that the sun shines on.)


She rises from her bed and no breath is in her
    breast,
To lean from out the casement that opens to the
    west.
    Is it sorrow or delight,
    That calls her in the night,
To draw her from the pillow of so tender-sweet
    a rest?
    Blessed is the day-dawn, and blessed is the sun,
    And blessed is the bride that the sun shines on.

Oh cold the buried love, oh colorless and wan!
(Blessed is the corpse that the rain rains on.)
  For her the pallid lip and for her the carven
    stone,
  For her the green fox-fire that lights the dead
    alone.
Oh living vow that looses the sheeted dead to
    run!
(Blessed is the corpse that the rain rains on.)


She rises from her sleep and the graven tablets
    stir;
She rises and she goes, for the vow is calling
    her,
  And the dampness of the rain
  Soothes the rigour of her pain—
Oh sad rain that weeps from the fringes of the fir!
  Nevermore at bridegroom's side shall lie down
    his vanished bride,
  For the death-in-life has clasped her that to
    love-in-death had died!

  *' Blessed is the bride that the sun shines on.*
  *Blessed is the corpse that the rain rains on.*

# PALE LEAVES AND LILIES.

# THE LOST SONG.

In sleep I hear it oftenest;
  Yet sometimes, failing, half-divine,
From the dusk purple of the west,
  It slants across some mood of mine.

Like far-off perfume of dead flowers—
  Like some dream face that, less and less,
Down long, pale memory-halls of ours,
  Fades dimmer till it vanishes.

Why do my eyes grow weakly wet?
  Why do my lips grow tremulous?
I cannot tell, and yet—and yet—
  I know that it was always thus.

# THERE IS A LITTLE ROSE TREE IN MY HEART.

There is a little rose tree in my heart,
   A little pink-tipped rose tree, dear, for you.
Sweet bud blooms growing in a place apart,
   Whose patch of sky is always warm and blue.

There is a little rose tree in your heart,
   A little, tender rose tree, dear, for me.
From its shy leaves fair perfumes take their start;
   To it comes every singing bird and bee.

Dear, let us pluck these roses, you and I.
   They know no canker and no thorny dart—
Each bud a kiss, each falling leaf a sigh!
   There is a little rose tree in my heart.

# I CANNOT TELL HOW MUCH.

I cannot tell how much,
  In these light, latter days,
Is hung upon her touch,
  Or little laughing ways.
For she is spring and song
  And light and inner-glow,
  And everything I know
    Seems mine but for her sake.
But this I know: If wrong
    And pain should come, nor spare
  The roses in her cheek,
    The gold that's in her hair—
If all the light were gone
  From out her loving look,
Still would my love sing on
  Like water in a brook.

I cannot tell how much,
  In this late afternoon,

Is love's own love-light, such
  As trembles through love's June.
For now for many a day
  She has been all to me,
  My sunshine and my sea,
    My forest and my flower.
But this I know: I pray
      For her where'er I rest,
      And in every waking hour,
        With the heart-beat in my breast.
And if all the light were gone
  From all life's laughing look,
Still would my love sing on
  Like water in a brook.

# SMILES AND TEARS.

Dearest, when you stand and smile,
   You are all a woman wise,
With a woman's wit and wile,
   With a woman's mouth and eyes.

Then I love you as my own,
   Calm, and level-eyed, serene,
With a passion sober grown,
   As my lady and my queen.

Ah, but dearest, when you weep,
   All the woman and the years
Slip away and go to sleep
   And the child wakes up in tears.

Then, sweetheart, I see but this—
   Just a small, bright head to feel
'Neath my cheek—my child to kiss
   With a little heart to heal.

# TO HER.

I sometimes think that if her hair
    Were not so fair and not so gold—
So less than gold, so more than fair,
    So meshed with odours manifold,

    That I would see in it the gold
        Of her fine soul (no lustre less!)
    Till my flush fancying, grown bold,
        Would dream it into loveliness.

I sometimes think that if her eyes
    Were not so wise and not so sweet—
So woman-sweet, so maiden-wise,
    And lashed with wilfulness complete,

    That I would look thro' their grey guise
        To her clear soul that glasses there—
    (But I am glad for her deep eyes.
        And oh, I'm glad for her gold hair!)

# A TRAVELER BY DAY.

Death, when you come at last
    To steal my life away,
Draw not down at dawn hour,
    When skies are opal-grey.
Knock not at duskfall,
    When clouds are purple-furled,
But come at nooning when the sun
    Is warm on all the world.

So shall I see clear
    Whither I embark.
So shall my soul not
    Slip into the dark.
So shall I not go
    In fearfulness of night,
But know, if I must leave her lone,
    I leave her in the light!

# THE PHILTRE.

If I cannot have her,
Never hold her, never move her,
  If her sweet, white body
Leans for another lover—
    Then let me forget
    That I ever held her face
        Between my tear-wet hands!
        May I see her where she stands,
      With the misty violet
    Of her eyes gone from its place!
May I see her draw her hair
    Lustreless across her brow,
That which golden was and rare
    Holding pallor now!


If I cannot press her,
Never kiss her nor caress her,
  If for her love-murmurings
Another one shall bless her—

Then my soul be blind
To all her loveliness!
  Let both my eyes be dim
  To breast, and waist, and limb!
Whatever grace I find,
May it fade less and less!
But the charms I so shall miss,
Richer, rarer than they were,
May they still frame round her kiss,
As is meet for her!

# THIS IS HOW SHE CAME TO ME.

This is how she came to me—
  With tremulous throbbing of her throat,
With lips that shook uncertainly
    And breast that fluttered like a bird,
  With eyes where love was all afloat
    And voice the sweetest ever heard.
In all the world were only we—
And this is how she came to me.

This is how she went away—
  With still hands folded on her breast
So like a little child might pray,
    With silent lips laid close and sweet
  And smiling to me through her rest;
    White lilies laid about her feet,
The promise of a further day—
And this is how she went away.

# THE FLOWER.

A flower bloomed in a desert grey.
Small comfort came to him by day.
Yet he drooped not beneath the blue,
But held pale petals up for dew.
A thousand times he dreamed of rain
(And, waking, wept to sleep again)
Which a fair, feathered cloud, gold-dim,
Had promised him!   Had promised him!

The flower bloomed in the desert white.
Small comfort came to him by night.
The sand blew choking.   One by one
His petals fell down in the sun.
So, dreaming still, he died.   And then
(When he could never drink again)
The rain came which the cloud, gold-dim,
Had promised him!   Had promised him!

# DEATH'S DISGUISE.

### (H. C. B.)

O Death, when from the dark you lean
   Toward her eyes and her sweet hair,
Come with no menace in your mien,
   And bring no face of horror there!

(Because so long since I have passed—
   Tho' not to go I was so fain—
And may not hold her at the last
   To kiss away the parting pain.)

Come to her when the sunlight dips,
   No grisly shape or weird surprise,
To smile upon her with my lips
   And gaze upon her with my eyes.

So may she, with her fainting breath,
   Naught knowing any sob or tear,
Stretching tired arms to you, dear Death,
   Kiss your white cheek without a fear.

# UNFORGOT.

Even in the fever-heat of noon,
   Sweet, who lie where stately winds are walking;
Even 'neath the sultry sailing moon,
   I hear you talking.

When the pave is throbbing with the heat,
   Dear, when all my weary toil is sleeping;
When at night I rest my tired feet,
   I hear your weeping.

My soul's sky is misty with sad rain,
   Love, whom never life could fashion dearer;
Day and night unspeakable the pain
   To hold you nearer!

# THE PATH.

Sobbing a little, holding tight my hand,
She slipped away into the lampless land,
Half fearing, half content to see the smile
My poor lips tried to comfort her awhile.
So out into the ever dark.   Ah, me!
It was so dark for such dear eyes to see!

Not mine to know the touch of her God's love,
Or the kind face she sometimes babbled of.
Mine but to sit and wait the opened door
And the long path she trod along before.
(I said she would not weary, then) but oh,
It was so far for such small feet to go!

# SHADOWS.

The firelight shadows tremble silently.
   (Shadow and real—they fall about us two.)
Oh am I but a wandering dream of me?
   And are you but a wistful dream of you?

Sometimes it seems the shadows are the real;
   The real seems sometimes faint and shadowy
     grown.
So wondrous true the dreams I used to feel,
   Such wondrous dreaming all that is my own!

For I have all the wonder of my dream;
   Too rich, too strange, too purple to be true!
And the dream's wonder dazes, till I seem
   To be but dreaming now this dream of you.

The firelight shadows fall about us two.
   (Shadow and real—they mingle endlessly.)
Oh are you but a wistful dream of you?
   And am I but a wandering dream of me?

# THE OPENED DOOR.

I cannot see you by the gleams
    That noonward blaze the weary sky,
But oh, you come to me in dreams
    And clasp me where I lie.

I cannot reach you with the kiss
    That trembles ever like a song
On my lips' portal—ah, it is
    A wanderer waiting long.

A weary traveler at the sill,
    Forbid by iron bolt and chain,
Who, shivering comfortless, must still
    Wait on in dark and rain.

Is it a madness, little one?
    Is it a fond and fevered touch
Of foolish love the daylight sun
    Laughs at for caring much?

Or are my dreams a truer thing
   Than all earth-fancies?   Does your breath
Light, spirit-drawn, stretch whispering
   Across the void of death?

And does your love still longer stay
   Subtle, fine-strung and tender-wise,
Ungrasped in my dull, grosser day,
   To kiss my tired eyes?

## MEETING.

When I am free-foot, quit of the mold
    When the outer air is my wandering place,
When my eyes are closed to the ways of old
    And I and my star stand face to face—

Somewhere, somehow, out of the dark,
    Out of the shadows that hold my dear,
When I come and call, oh she will hark
    And answer suddenly, " I am here! "

" Here! "   And the shadows shall start away
    And I and my dear in the world of men
Shall spring together beyond the day
    And there, in the long light, kiss again.

# APRIL.

I would not care what day might bring,
   I would not reck how night might fall,
If she stayed for me with the spring,
   To be my all in all!

I would not care—I would but know
   That all that happiness might be,
While I was worn and wanting so,
   Was with her, waiting me.

But now, whatever day may bring
   And howsoe'er the night may fall,
I shall not find her with the spring,
   Nor greet her e'er at all.

# CYTHEREA.

Here where the grasses blow
  She lies at rest.
For her to slumber so
  Is for the best.

Love and the light are past
  From her young eyes
In other lore at last
  So over-wise.

Hers now the freer air,
  Hers the glad sky;
All of our pity's care
  Now may go by!

Hers the fall's secret is
  Of ferns and firs.
Held not for any kiss
  Those lips of hers.

All the wide summer's page,
  All lilies say,
Has been her heritage
  Many a day.

Speak not of ways where went
  Her careless feet;
What ill her living lent
  Now is all sweet!

Rare, too, and fine she was
  Once, as a rose.
All that she missed with us
  Here, now she knows.

Say not it is too late
  For a last dower.
Sow not a thorn in hate.
  Leave her a flower!

# COMPENSATION.

Dearest, for me the breath of flowers,
  The morning breaking rosy-wise.
For you the red worm through the hours
  And mold upon your eyes.

For you the earth smell and the rain,
  The wan roots writhing overhead;
For me an ever-sobbing pain
  And few, few words you said.

For me the light pulsating waste,
  For me the noisy wrinkling sea;
For you all silences are laced,
  All darks wove endlessly.

And yet I would that I could lie
  In darks and silences as deep,
Where drawn lips can not laugh or sigh,
  Nor dusty eyes can weep.

If I but knew that you o'erhead,
  Beneath the sky's caressing smile,
Went sometimes sorrowing for the dead
  As I do all the while.

# THE SLAVE.

I never dream a dream or sad or sweet,
  Walking the pave or sleeping in my bed,
But somehow, hastening ever with light feet,
  Her love gleams like a little star ahead.

I never carve a phrase or trace a line,
  Or smooth a wayward verse, or coax a song,
But through the struggling word this ear of mine
  Hears her voice whisper, murmurous and long.

I cannot lead my mind where she is not!
  I cannot come in body where she is!
Dear mistress of my every theme and thought,
  Whose living lips my lips can never kiss!

A fond and eager slave, I bless the chain,
  Lest I, left lonely with a lesser art,
Should dream and, dreaming, miss the bitter pain
  To run and lay my head upon her heart.

# RED LEAVES AND ROSES.

# SEVEN.

Seven stars in the sky
  And the broad sea under.
With seven loves she loves me,
  With love surpassing wonder.

The love of the child for faith.
  The love of the youth for winning;
The love of the lover, fearful, bold—
  The love of the nun that's sinning.

The woman's love for love,
  The love of the maid for heaven;
The mother-love—and this is last.
  So!  Her loves are seven.

Seven stars overhead.
  With the seven loves I bought her!
And the seven stars in the sky
  Are a snake of fire in the water.

# THE LOVERS' CREED.

The heart from its heart, all the passions and tears
      And time that can cover
      The wounds of a lover,
Can keep, while the fates hold the struggling years
      To warring and winning
      And praying and sinning.

        *Women are women.*
        *Men are men.*
    *Love will come to its own again.*

But soul from its soul, for the space of a breath,
      Nor falsehood nor feature,
      Creator nor creature,
The transport of living, the spasm of death—
      None can dissever
      Forever and ever.

        *Women are women.*
        *Men are men.*
    *Love will come to its own again.*

# DESTINY.

Two roses red within a garden grew,
And I was one rose and the other you.
And all the yellow day we sighed to show
What all the purple night we wept to know.

Two tall pines stood upon a rock-cliff high,
And you were one pine and the other I.
And all the winds our murmuring bore along,
And all the weak waves wept to hear our song.

Two seabirds grey above the beaches flew,
And I was one bird and the other you.
We sought through all the weary, weary West.
A-wing we met and singing, built our nest.

# THE STILL REMEMBERED.

A lover once sought thro' cities of tombs
  For his darling the White Plague would not
    spare
And delved in their dust and their vacant glooms,
  While madness grew in his heart's despair
    To make of the years but a shadowy haze
That wrapped about him and hid her there.
Till one day, as he groped dim catacombs,
    In a niche long hid, on a sudden outrolled
  From a rotting coffin of rosewood rare,
    Tawny-flecked, russet-brown, in a tangle of
      gold,
  A billowy sweep of the flame-washed hair
    That only his darling, of all the world,
  Had braided so long and so wondrous fair.
      The tresses had grown and spread and
      curled
    Like amber lace, laid fold on fold,
  Or beaten metal beyond compare.

Into the dust had vanished the rest—
The mist and the violet dew of her eyes,
  The sweet, straight limbs, the round, sweet
    breast,
And the smile that was tender and kind and wise.
All of her glorious soul was mold—
  Only the hair he had wound and kissed
A thousand thousand times untold,
  Curling and clasping round his wrist
For his lips to touch and his hands to hold!
  But then, as he gazed, it dropped, was
    rust,
Its bright dun faded, its sheen grew old,
  And all in an instant, it fell to dust.


So it came that he passed to the summer air,
  Free from the chains of the grave and its
    cold,
And blessing this one last kiss of her hair
  That was living and loving and dear and
    gold.

# THE VOID.

Oh the daylight, yellow, lonely!
  Oh the dark with its chilly touch!
Sweet, the day would be golden, only—
  Could I forget to grieve so much.

Could I but think of you as waiting
  (Not as wandering through the hours),
Night would be more than weary hating;
  Dark would blossom in fiery flowers.

Oh, I have guessed it, hoped it, prayed it,
  Cried for it, bled for it, died for it, dear!
Only to know—to *know* death made it
  Only our door to a further " here! "

Never a whisper, breath of you dreaming,
  Never a cold, soft touch at night!
Never a sound or a sense of seeming,
  Never a shadow to bless my sight!

Come to me, dear, if ever so fleeting
  The one little touch or clasp or kiss!
Life is more than the red heart's beating.
  Come to me, sweetheart! Tell me this!

# THE WEARY HOUSE.

Not costly wine or meat I pray, O Lord,
(Not gold or gems to comfort my sad heart!)
    Only a crust—so it be from her hand,
    For I am blind and in a strange, blind land
And sadness evermore must crown my board.
Give me no cruel jest of food, dear Lord!

Not for fine gold or shining gems, O Lord,
(Not rugs or tapestries of cunning art!)
    But for the leaping yellow of her hair
    When the sun warms it and the happy air
Gives it all light and laughter it has stored.
What are the gold or gems to me, dear Lord?

Not for rich rugs or tapestries, O Lord,
(Give me but her, and let my life's joys start!)
    O looms of threaded sunshine!  These be less
    Than the sweet lines of one pale, figured dress
In which she stands before me like a sword.
Let this come to my weary house, dear Lord!

Give me but her—-but her, I pray, O Lord!
(Food, gold or house, oh, they are little part!)
   Only her slender body for my touch,
   Her lips to kiss, her love to love so much!
With all her blood were tangled joys outpoured!
All else is naught; so mock me not, dear Lord!

# THE BURNING BUSH.

Last week the fields were mossed and green,
  Musing on what they knew of her;
The straight-boled poplars seemed to lean
  To filch a fading view of her.
The sentinel-bush beside the hedge,
  Drooped low with grace it bought of her,
Shook, like my heart, from edge to edge
  At sight of her and thought of her.

Now, now the fields are brown and fey
  That used to dream so much of her;
The solemn hedge-row, gaunt and grey,
  Is pale with frosty touch of her.
The sentinel-bush by which she came,
  That blushed the darling fate of her,
Like my red heart, is all aflame
  With love of her and hate of her!

# "AND ONE SHALL BE TAKEN."

Kissing me, missing me, folded down
   Nightly her lids over eyes of grey—
All of the labouring left for the town,
   All of the toil and the work-a-day.

Kissing me, missing me, still in sleep;
   Breath like a little tired child abed.
All of the angels her flower soul keep!
   All of earth's troubles go over her head!

Kissing me, missing me, waver so
   The cloud-pale eyelids whose pulse is gone;
All of the quick blood that danced, running slow,
   The pulse-shake dulling away to the dawn.

Kissing me, missing me—is there a bliss
   Somewhere, otherwhere, when she shall wake,
Something as splendid to stand for my kiss?
   Give it not, Death, for sweet King Love's sake!

# NEVER AGAIN.

Never again—ah, never again for me
    The new sun's lances shooting joy a-land!
Never again, soft, seasoned by the sea,
    Her little lips upon my sun-brown hand!
Never, I know, can olden idyls be—
Never again—ah, never again for me!

Never again—ah, never again for her
    The whitening shells, the waves' wide, watery
       noon!
Never again the whisper of the fir
    Low lisping to the yellow, sailing moon!
Never may lights and darks be all they were—
Never again—ah, never again for her!

Never again—ah, never again for us
    The same joy-day, love-night and clinging touch!
Never again shall we two, lip-linked thus,
    Wonder if ever loving held so much!
Never shall aught be aught of what it was—
Never again—ah, never again for us!

# GUILT.

One day I trod upon a heart—
    Set heel upon it where it lay.
My shoe was purple and my art
    Could wash the stain away.

It shed a perfume like a rose
    Crushed between breasts of lovers pale,
Or like the bruised wistaria does
    Beneath a summer hail.

I washed my shoe within a brook
    And dried it on the burnished grass.
The water laughed up at my look,
    But the bent sky was brass.

I passed again along the way
    When the rich fallow evening swooned;
I saw the same heart where it lay.
    It never showed a wound!

But as I walked, my nostrils filled
   Full of that rose scent, over-fair,
Like a fine Persian attar, spilled
   Far-faint on heavy air.

I flung away the purple shoe
   And naked-footed took the sod;
But every footprint, well I knew,
   Smelt guiltily to God.

# FORSAKEN.

I used to pray—I used to pray
   Each evening when the day was dim,
   That all things good might come to him—
That every joy that makes us gay,
   For his heart's lips might over-brim,
And blessings crowd his way!

I used to pray—I used to pray
   Each morning when the sun was red
   And its first shafts lay on my bed,
That all his summer might be May
   And all his winter comforted,
So long as love might stay!

I used to pray—I used to pray
   The same sweet praying o'er and o'er.
   Now I have double-locked the door
Of my lips, so glad yesterday,
   And I shall pray no more, no more,
As I was used to pray!

# SINCE I DIED.

Since I died her face has been paling.
  I cannot see, but I know—I know!
Little such love could linger, failing
  Answering passion to kiss it so!

How I have wrestled and fought and prayed me
  (Knowing that she would come to my side)
Only to stay—to stay where they laid me—
  Since that curious night I died!

Fingers stretching and voices calling—
  I am restless and I would run.
Riotous footfalls—hear them falling?
  How such beckoning will tempt one!

But I will not go! I will not listen!
  I will lie and wait in the dark for my dear.
Perhaps, if I were to run, new-risen,
  I could not remember the way back here!

Some near day, in the rain-washed weather,
   They will bring her here in a dress of white,
And we shall lie and whisper together—
   Ever together by day and night!

She never knew it—never has guessed it—
   Never has thought that death was a lie!
Never has dreamed how I kissed it and blessed it—
   But then she will know what it means to die.

I will show her how not to surrender—
   Never to run with the riot and stir,
For oh, she will far rather rest in the tender
   Passion a dead man holds for her!

Lightning Source UK Ltd.
Milton Keynes UK
UKHW01f1909210818
327592UK00015B/1043/P